A COLLISION WITH PURPOSE

In Pursuit Of Purpose

DR. LAXLEY W. STEPHENSON

Published by Victorious You Press™
Charlotte NC, USA

TITLE: A COLLISION WITH PURPOSE

First Printed: 2023

Editor: Lynn Braxton

Book Cover Designer Ottoreece Melhado (Shella TopStar)

ISBN: (eBook) 978-1-959719-23-6

ISBN: Paperback 978-1-959719-22-9

ISBN: Hardcover 978-1-959719-28-1

Library of Congress Control Number: 2023919979

Printed in the United States of America

For details email joan@victoriousyoupress.com
or visit us at www.victoriousyoupress.com

Contents

DEDICATION

This book is dedicated to the loving memory of my cherished mother, Winsome Mae Marjorie Vassall, my father, Ronald Stephenson, and my dear friend, Dr. Delorese Ambrose, whose warmth and wisdom illuminated the pages of my life. You were the lighthouse that guided me through stormy seas, providing strength, love, and unyielding support. Your memory remains engraved in my heart, your spirit still embraces me in my darkest moments.

To my precious grandchildren, Kanaan Loxley Stephenson and Annalise Yvonne Nala Foster, you have brought boundless joy and light into my life. Your curiosity, laughter, and endless zest for life inspire me each day. Through your eyes, I glimpse the wonder of the world anew. Your presence will always be a beacon of hope and love, reminding me of the beauty of life's simplest moments. This book is a testament to my love and commitment to you both.

To my wonderful daughters, Tremaine Stephenson and Kiana Stephenson, who have consistently been my pillars of strength and encouragement, I am eternally thankful for your love, patience, and understanding. Your belief in my work and your steadfast presence in my life have been a source of solace and motivation, enabling me to achieve this milestone.

I dedicate this book to all of you, whose immeasurable love and influence have shaped not only these pages but also the very essence of who I am. Your spirits live on in the words that follow, immortalized in the hearts and minds of all those who find solace and inspiration within these pages.

ACKNOWLEDGEMENT

I am filled with immense gratitude as I reflect on the many individuals who have contributed to the creation of this book. Each person has played a unique and vital role, leaving an indelible mark on both the pages and my heart.

First and foremost, I would like to express my heartfelt appreciation to Miss Donna Thompson, contributing author, whose expertise, guidance, and unwavering support have been instrumental in bringing this project to fruition. Her passion and dedication have inspired me throughout the writing process, and I am genuinely grateful for her invaluable contributions.

I am grateful for the unwavering support and love of my siblings: my brother, Martin Thompson and his wife, Joan Thompson; my sisters, Geraldine Palomino, Paulette Ricketts, Hope Johnson, and Andrea McIntosh; my nieces, Dee Dee Thompson, Renae Lee-Rogers, Minieve West, Sevana West, Elianna West, Arianna Rickets, Schnelle Acevedo, Sheree Smith, Alisa Palomino, and Lorraine Green; my nephews, Dwight Ricketts, Martin Thompson Jr., Andrew Peterkin, Jordon Thompson, Izaiah Lee, Zyaire West, and Caleb Lee; my cousins Grace Laing-Moore, Donna Laing, Collville Laing, Kissock Laing, Courtney Laing, Joan Laing, Collis Peart, Colleen Locke, Wayne Davis, and Gayaan Wilson.

Your encouragement, patience, and unwavering faith in my capabilities are the driving forces that kept me going during the most challenging times. I could not have done this without you. I am eternally grateful for your steadfast support.

Thank you to my friends, James Laird, Daniel Laird, Barbara Dunn, Melissa Blair, Brinkman Malcolm, Marlene Malcolm, Emrol G. Edwards, Simone M. Mitchell, Marva Smith, Ottoreece Melhado (Shella TopStar), Garfield McCook, Dr. Iglika Kirilov, Lexi Johnson, Ann Marie Bailey, Garfield James, Ryan Keating, Rica Newell, Claudy Eugene, Donovan Mercurius, Dr. Binzie Roy Davidson, and Dr. Cecelia Lynch-Mitchell. Your camaraderie, advice, and shared experiences have immensely enriched my life and played an integral role in shaping the ideas and perspectives presented in this book.

My heartfelt thanks go to the study's numerous collaborators who form this work's foundation. This book would not have been possible without your willingness to share your stories, insights, and experiences. Your contributions have deepened my understanding and enriched the lives of countless others who will read these pages.

I sincerely thank my publisher, Victorious You Press, whose enthusiasm for the project and commitment to its success has been indispensable. Your trust, guidance, and expertise have been invaluable in transforming a collection of thoughts and ideas into a cohesive and engaging narrative that I am proud to share with the world.

Lastly, I wish to acknowledge the reader whose curiosity and desire for knowledge have led you to explore these pages. I am honored and grateful for the opportunity to share my work with you, and I hope it will inspire, inform, and enrich your life in some way.

To all who have touched my life and contributed to the creation of this book, I offer my deepest gratitude and dedicate this work to you. Your presence in my life has been a gift.

FOREWORD

In the realm of personal growth and self-improvement, a few shining stars illuminate the path for others. Dr. Laxley W. Stephenson is undeniably one of these guiding lights, a beacon of hope for individuals from all walks of life. It is both an honor and a privilege to introduce you to the transformative work of Dr. Stephenson.

Dr. Stephenson's words resonate deeply with the human spirit in a world filled with uncertainty and challenges. Through his remarkable storytelling and relatable approach, he has the rare gift of connecting with diverse audiences, from career professionals to small business owners, entrepreneurs, and faith-based spiritual leaders. His message transcends boundaries, offering invaluable tools and strategies to embrace our situations, find meaning, and embark on a journey of finding purpose.

Dr. Stephenson's impact extends far beyond the pages of his books and the podiums of his speaking engagements. His unwavering dedication to philanthropy is a testament to his commitment to helping others. As the founder of Global Humanity Network, Inc., a non-profit organization aimed at empowering underprivileged youth, he showcases his belief in the potential of every individual to lead purpose-driven lives. Through this noble endeavor, he exemplifies the principles he preaches, proving that the power of purpose can uplift entire communities.

As an educator, Dr. Stephenson combines his spiritual and natural gifts to guide us toward our purpose, helping us discover the profound connection between our inner selves and the outer world. His work is a testament to the power of storytelling, and his ability to inspire others to share their own stories is nothing short of remarkable. Dr. Stephenson's impact reaches far and wide, touching the lives of individuals from every corner of the globe. His words resonate deeply with those seeking to find their purpose and unlock their full potential.

A Collision with Purpose perfectly encapsulates Dr. Stephenson's mission to change the way we perceive ourselves and our connection to our life's calling. This book is not just an invitation; it's a call to action. It urges us to look in the mirror and confront the potential that lies within us, encouraging us to do the necessary work to become the best version of ourselves.

As you embark on this literary journey with Dr. Laxley Stephenson, you are in the company of a visionary, a mentor, and a catalyst for personal growth. The collision with purpose that awaits you within these pages is a collision with your potential, and Dr. Stephenson serves as the guiding force to help you navigate this path.

So, embrace the wisdom within these pages, for they hold the keys to unlocking your true purpose and propelling you toward the person you are destined to become. Dr. Laxley Stephenson's work is not just a testament to the power of words; it's a testament to the power within you.

I have a profound respect and admiration for the incredible work of Dr. Laxley Stephenson.

Joan T Randall
The Author's Midwife. Founder & CEO Victorious You Press

INTRODUCTION

"In life, we all experience pain and suffering in different forms, whether physical, emotional, or spiritual, leaving us feeling lost. But what if I told you that pain, defiance, and destiny could unlock your true calling in life."

Dr. Laxley W. Stephenson

Walking your path may involve overcoming obstacles and facing hard-to-embrace truths about yourself and the world around you. Yet the rewards are well worth the effort. When you have a goal or aim, you will experience a deeper fulfillment and meaning in both your life and the lives of others.

At its core, *A Collision With Purpose: In Pursuit of Purpose*, is about hope, healing, and the human spirit's power to overcome adversity and find its calling. It aims to inspire and motivate readers to embrace their struggles pursue their unique reason for being, and use it as a force for good.

A Collision With Purpose offers a compassionate exploration of the ability to overcome significant obstacles. It will resonate with individuals from all walks of life, supplying tools and strategies to embrace their reason for existence and transform their lives.

As you explore these pages, you will encounter various perspectives and insights from those who intentionally sought and found their reasons for living. Be open-minded to learn from the experiences of this diverse group of individuals on their journey to uncover their unique purpose.

Embark on a journey of self-discovery and exploration as you seek to identify what drives you in life. The path to this realization is unique to each individual, requiring courage, honesty, and a willingness to embrace change. Through others' lived experiences, be prepared to uncover insights to guide your own journey.

May you find the courage, wisdom, and guidance to reveal your true calling and lead a life of intention and meaning. And may your discoveries impact not only you but many others. *A Collision With Purpose* will be your guide and inspiration as you navigate this quest.

Be courageous in following your calling, take quiet moments to listen, engage in self-reflection, maintain your curiosity, and seek lasting and meaningful relationships. Remember that your success is founded on your capacity to continuously examine yourself, identify gaps, and translate your words into actions and results. You are Significant! Blessings Always!

SECTION I

Pain To Purpose

Pain to Purpose is a transformative journey that begins in suffering and adversity, only to emerge into a brighter, more meaningful existence. It is a path where the trials and tribulations of life become the resources for personal growth and a newfound sense of direction. At the onset, pain can feel like an unrelenting storm, tearing through the fabric of one's soul. However, within these moments of despair, individuals often discover their true resilience and inner strength.

As the journey unfolds, pain starts to take on a different meaning. It becomes a catalyst for change, a powerful force that propels people toward their calling. Turning pain into purpose requires introspection, healing, and a conscious decision to use one's experiences to impact the world positively—encouraging individuals to embrace their pain as the foundation on which they forge their purpose and forever transform their lives with newfound meaning and a profound sense of fulfillment.

Dr. Laxley W. Stephenson

A Tragedy Unfolded

"Purpose Was Unfolding; It Had Found Me In
A Place That Had Become Foreign."

Paula Campbell

Paula Thornton-Campbell is a wife and mother. An accomplished writer with several published articles, including Essence magazine. She is an advocate for mental and emotional health. In her spare time, she enjoys spending time with her grandsons.

My Early Years

My early childhood was not a typical one. My mother and father raised my nieces and nephews more like their own children, to be mild-mannered, I learned early on to share and to be compassionate, and that is what I want to be remembered for—my compassion.

Purpose Defined

The definition of Purpose is knowing that you are called to do an assignment, which can be divine or practical. I think that Purpose begins the moment we are born. As we grow older, Purpose begins to enlighten us about what we're supposed to do in life. The divine Purpose could be your ministerial Purposes, such as a pastor, the clergy, a nun, or evangelism. The Practical Purpose is the thinking and actions of doctors, teachers, social advocates, the media, or anything that impacts society. If someone comes to you, and when they leave, they are better off than when they first came to you, then that was your Purpose.

Importance of Purpose

It is extremely important to understand your Purpose because our Purpose influences our behaviors, actions, and feelings. I have had a sense of knowing what I was supposed to do from a very early age. I love writing, and that's always been my passion. It is something that came very naturally to me, and it influenced my behavior. It influenced the grades I received in school. Therefore, I did well in English literature. I have gone on to write poetry, participated in spoken word, and written books aligning with my Purpose. It is important to know what your Purpose is because it's going to influence everything that you do in life. Purpose always circles back around. You cannot get over it, you can't get under it. It will come back around to you some way, somehow. It is an instinct; you know that you are supposed to do something. It is the burning in your belly.

My Purpose

I am a mental health advocate. I wrote a bestselling anthology entitled Mommy's Mental Health. It was number one on Amazon within a few days. I bring awareness to mental health to erase the stigma surrounding it. We live in a society of uncertainty, especially since COVID, which has impacted people's mental health and is a topic of many discussions. You hear it in the media, you see it on social media, and we see it in the news, and we are aware of it with celebrities.

Around 2016, I spoke at a women's conference about my battle with depression and post traumatic stress disorder (PTSD) after I witnessed the murder of my sister when I was seventeen. That incident played a very intricate role in my life. I could not make those thoughts disappear, and I was ashamed to talk about it in the beginning because I felt different. I did not feel normal.

So, I began to speak more about depression and how real it is, and now in society, you hear more and more people talking about it. It has just become something very passionate for me to shed light on. To turn down the volume on it creates too much silence surrounding mental health. The statistics show that 50 million people battle depression or mental health challenges per year. One in three people will commit suicide every fifteen minutes. That number is just astronomical. It is crazy to me that we live in the twenty-first century, and people must hide behind their emotions. I want to help break that stigma. I know I can't do it alone. If I can leave a situation better than it was before I got there, then I have done my job; then I have fulfilled my Purpose.

Life Events Informs my Purpose

Confronted by a tragic event in my life, I had no choice. I had to move forward. I had to keep going. So that situation, as horrific as it was, served as a platform for me to tell people that bad things will happen. We can't control that. But you can go on and move forward and find some good in it. The good that I see is I can speak to women through their purpose, passion, and pain to encourage them to keep moving forward despite the atrocities that might occur in their lives.

My Book/My Work

My book is titled Mommy's and Mental Health, an anthology of women who battle mental health issues ranging from postpartum depression to post-traumatic stress disorder. It entails the stories of twelve other women and one man who have overcome astronomical mental illnesses and have gone on to do great things in life. They move forward. They did not let it stop them. I share my story of sitting in my closet with my husband's gun to my head because I didn't know what was happening to me when I began to have flashbacks and deep bouts of depression; I did not want to live. And one day when I was in the closet with my husband's gun to my head, I remember hearing the voice of God so clearly telling me, "No, you won't do this! You will go forward. You will live. You can make it through this." So, the book is a powerful tool with coping strategies—each woman talks about the coping strategies they use. In my anthology, I had the privilege of sharing my story with twelve other women. And I am very proud to have been a part of that project.

Impact of the Pursuit of My Purpose

Mental health issues affect so many, it's my goal to let people know there is no shame in getting help. There is no shame in saying that I am stuck. I need to *know how* to move forward. I need to *learn how* to move forward. I need someone to tell me that I am not alone and that this is as real as a heart attack or a gut problem. It is an illness of the mind. Like when the body gets sick, there's so much evidence to show how it affects the rest of the body. Depression can lead to heart disease, gut, skin, and hair issues. Sometimes my depression was so bad that I lost my hair, but it grew back.

Alignment With My Purpose

Being aligned with your Purpose means paying attention to the things that happen in your life, who comes in and out of your life, and how you are catapulted in your plights in life. Success leaves clues, and so does Purpose. Very early on in my life, writing was instrumental in getting to where I wanted to be. So that was a clue for me. I knew that whatever I did in life would involve writing. Yes, I did have a side job in real estate and other ventures, but ultimately my Purpose was to write. It was not until after my sister was murdered that I realized that event gave me a platform to write about.

So, it is important to know that when you align yourself for a Purpose, pay attention to the clues that come into your life. And when you are walking in your Purpose, you are in alignment. Things fall into place. Still, I believe it is divine for me to connect with Dr. Stephenson and have this conversation about Purpose because it aligns with the work I am doing in my life. I don't believe that Purpose can be avoided. Whether you get off the bandwagon or get back on, at some point, you will come full circle back to what your Purpose is supposed to be. It is in you.

Purpose Full Circle

Of all the things that Purpose means to me, the most profound is how I experienced it coming full circle, back to where it all began in my hometown of Durham, North Carolina. About one year ago, I hit an emotional and mental wall. It was as if every hurt, sorrow, disappointment, and loss had returned to destroy me. Every day was as if I was living November 26, 1985, all over again—the year my sister was murdered. I cried, screamed, and wailed uncontrollably. I couldn't eat; sleep was my only escape. Then, I found a doctor who diagnosed me with severe PTSD and severe depression. Her fresh set of eyes prescribed the right meds, and I began climbing my way out of the abyss.

Finally functioning, I caught up with an old high school friend I had not seen in twenty years. One look at her, and I could tell she was going through something. Her eyes were sunken and swollen, her clothes were disheveled, and her significant weight loss was evident. As we talked, she shared with me that she battled treatment-resistant depression. I listened as she spoke in between sobs. Then it hit me that what I had gone through personally was not only for me, but it was for someone else. Purpose was unfolding; it had found me in a place that had become foreign with a person who was foreign as well. While my friend and I talked, Purpose entered our conversation. As awful as my experience had been, its Purpose was freeing. I was able to let my friend know that she was no longer alone. I assured her that I understood and that she had my support. Tears streamed down her face as she seemed to breathe a sigh of relief. I was in awe of how Purpose was presenting itself after all the time that had gone by. It had come full circle, powerful and profound. Defying space and time, Purpose reigned.

Finding Purpose

First, pray and pay attention to that small still voice you are hearing. What is it telling you to do? What is it that makes you get up in the morning? What drives you? What is annoying? What do you know above all else? What volume is speaking the loudest to you? Pay attention to that. Write out your thoughts, both the positive, the negative, and everything in between. That is a good starting point for knowing what your Purpose is, if you're struggling. Pay attention to your gut instinct. What's gnawing at your gut? Intuition is your most powerful tool. You can't get away from it. So, pay attention to that feeling. Write it out. Pray it out. It is going to keep coming up, so you might as well jump on the bandwagon. And look deep within. It is that small, still voice that gnaws away at you. Sometimes you can't sleep at night because it's so loud.

Is Purpose a Topic of Discussion in Your Circle?

Well, for me, it is. I am a pastor's wife. And I have had to engage in women's ministry, and the first women's conference we had was entitled Empowering Women for their Purpose, their Passion, and their Pain. Finding your Purpose and being a topic of discussion is one that I have a passion for because I don't believe that the woman's place is always in the home raising kids all the time. You were created for a purpose, not to say that particular Purpose is bad. It's not. But I challenge women to pursue their passions as well as their Purpose. And they are all intertwined. So, Purpose is a topic of discussion in my conferences. I have one called the Couture Woman, where we talk about the Proverbs 31 woman who considers a field and buys it. She is a businesswoman, as well as a wife and mother. She's an entrepreneur.

So, Purpose is a big deal for me, especially given the platform I have with women. I encourage them to be the best overall person they can be, the best woman they can be so that they will have a joyful life, a life of meaning, a life filled with passion and Purpose.

The Role of Children

I relate to my grandsons, who are ten and six, by telling them to never settle. Complacency will keep you from striving to be the best person you can be. So, I tell them to always do their best and strive to achieve the very best in life. I always hone in on their skills. For example, my six-year-old grandson has a passion for dinosaurs. He can tell you about every dinosaur there is, what they eat, what they don't eat, and what their natural habitat is. In watching him, it was just amazing to see him have this much passion for something. He was only four years old when he developed it. He has every dinosaur that Target has on the shelf. So, I help him with that passion, in that pursuit. I don't know what he will turn out to be, but that is one of the clues to his Purpose. If we can pick up on those clues in children early on in life, we can help them achieve great things in their future.

For instance, the child that becomes a neurosurgeon, as a little boy or girl, they had knowledge or expressed interest in the brain, and someone took hold of them and said, "Okay, you have this interest, you have this passion. I am going to help you hone those skills to become a neurosurgeon." And that passion grew within them from the time they were a child to an adult.

As I said, Purpose leaves clues. It doesn't just pop up out of nowhere. It leaves clues from early on to adulthood.

Awareness in My Family About My Purpose

My Purpose is tied to writing. So, any time anyone in my family needs a paper written, or they need a poem for a funeral or a wedding, I am the one they call because they know that I'm a writer, and I will drop some skills on paper and put them in ink.

I am a real estate agent by trade. That's how I make my living. So, I had to learn how to incorporate writing into that. On the weekends when I wasn't showing homes, I would write poetry. I am always writing something because it's just in me. It aligns with who I am, and what I'm supposed to do. But I have to live, too, and I got to eat. So, I must go to work and make a living to feed my family. But that passion always circles back around. It comes full circle, always.

Walking In My Purpose

As I'm sitting here engaging in this conversation about Purpose, I am in awe because I was not expecting this to happen. Earlier, I wrote that I was part of the anthology, it was very satisfying and fulfilling. But as soon as that was done, I was thinking, *Okay, what's next? What am I going to do next? Where am I going to speak next? Who's going to call me next?* And when Kiana reached out to me and said that Dr. Stephenson wanted to do this interview with me, I said, "Okay, God, I hear you. I see what you are doing. This is truly my Purpose, and you are making a way for me to have a platform to speak on it." And so, it becomes overwhelming at times to see that Purpose is so real in my life. And I am walking it out.

My Final Thoughts About Purpose

Recognizing your Purpose requires you to pay attention to your intuition. Your intuition will never lie to you. It will always guide you and lead you where you're supposed to be. Pray first. Write everything out that you are feeling—the positive, the negative, the indifferent, the in-between. Write it out, and you'll always go right. If you trust your intuition, trust your gut. Trust that small, still voice that is so small, yet, so loud, and you won't go wrong. Pay attention to that small, still voice that is so loud you can't get away from it. When you get up and are struggling throughout the night, get up, write, get it on paper. Look at it the following day and do it again the next night. And the next night. And the next night. And it will become easier to recognize what your Purpose is. Trusting your intuition.

How Will I Fix This

"I saw there were not enough black women, black people, minorities, and biopic individuals in medicine. Who will do the work to fill those gaps, if not the people most closely affected by those gaps?"

Danielle Reid

Danielle Reid grew up in Gwinnett County in Georgia with an interest in the human condition and the diseases that plague us. At Emory University, she obtained a Bachelor of Science in Nursing (BSN), graduated Magna Cum Laude, worked for several years in the Neonatal Intensive Care unit at Northside Hospital in Atlanta. As a travel nurse to various states, Danielle became aware of the gaps in treatment for minorities. These experiences solidified her belief in the necessity of minority physicians in medicine. Determined to obtain her medical doctorate, she is enrolled with a full tuition scholarship at New York University Grossman Long Island School of Medicine, an expedited 3-year medical school, to address equity and gaps in internal medicine outcomes for minorities.

My Early Years

I recall my early childhood as carefree. There was a lot of structure that I can thank my mom for, which helps me in my current life as a registered nurse who specializes in neonatal intensive care. There was a lot of focus on school, studying, and sports. There was a lot of predictability; you come home from school, do your homework, and then we have dinner, after which it would be time for bed; of course, this was at a specific time. Even into young adulthood, my entire childhood still had that predictable structure.

I do recall being annoyed at how organized everything was. It was over the top. Of course, for any child, this would have been a normal feeling. I wanted to come home from school and sleep or nap. On Saturday mornings, my mom would wake us up at eight or nine and say, "Okay, it's Saturday; it's cleaning day." This was her expectation on Saturdays, and I would have to finish the chores before the fun stuff could start. Often, I would think, *Oh, my friends don't have to do things like this. They can do whatever they want, any time they wish.* So, I remember feeling that sort of childhood resentment and annoyance at that kind of thing. So much of it got internalized for me over the years. By the time I was in high school, I found myself creating structure for my life. Naturally, I would say, "I'm going to do this at this time, I'm going to work on this subject, and I'm going to watch TV." Even if no one was around, including my parents, it still felt like the right thing to do.

I carried that on through college and then through my working career. Now that I'm an adult, I appreciate that my early childhood had that much structure; it helped me in my adult life. It has helped me be more successful, So I'm grateful. Now it's just like part of my personality, and I love it. Instead of invoking anxiety, it gives me a sense of peace to be so organized and have an expectation of my days and weeks.

Purpose Defined

I assume that purpose subconsciously and unconsciously drives your actions, and your decision-making is a search for your purpose. Whether you have found it already or whether it's something that you're still looking for, there is something intrinsic that drives your actions. That's what your purpose is. This innate feeling of this is what I should do; this is a decision I should make.

Importance of Knowing Your Purpose

It is important to understand one's purpose and to bind yourself with that purpose but not to let it cause you too much anxiety in nailing it down. I see purpose as being fluid and changing throughout your life, and you may start, at one age, with a particular set of circumstances; then later find your purpose in something else. When you do see or discover it at a given stage in your life, it can be very fulfilling for you. The sense of fulfillment, calm, peace, ambition, whatever that purpose might provide, makes it important.

My Purpose

Defining my purpose now, as I see it, would be that I have many purposes for my current circumstance and future. There are many purposes that I might fulfill later in life versus where I am right now. What comes to mind, is my purpose for my family and my career and to be a provider or nurturer later in life. I feel a sense of responsibility to my family, and I want to support them emotionally, physically, socially, and financially in all these ways. So that's one of the purposes I have in my life as a daughter and sister. When I was younger and started my career as a nurse, I wanted that, but that has changed progressively. I have another purpose for my career that I'm still exploring. I'm going to be a Neonatal nurse, and I'm going to work on this with families. As a Neonatal nurse, you don't just work with the baby, right? As a pediatric Nurse, you usually work with the entire family, anyone who comes to visit; you're in service to a whole family, which feels very fulfilling.

As I progressed in my career as a nurse and in my education, I learned more about minority medicine, disparities in healthcare for minorities, such as Blacks, Hispanics, and Native Americans. I could see in real-time the effects the healthcare system and society have on minorities. This made me more drawn to nail down the direction of being in service to minority health. So now, as I'm moving towards becoming a physician, I feel like it's my purpose to get involved and be a change-maker when it comes to health care and minority medicine, both on the individual level for patients that I see, as well as on a macro level regarding policy making, curriculum, and education of the health care system and how that impacts minority medicine.

That's where I'm going in my career, purpose-wise. My other purpose when it comes to this is more personal. I have a purpose and an intention to have a fun, fulfilling life. I include self-care as part of my purpose. Another aspect of my purpose is to find ways to be happy and have fun in my current position. I intentionally make decisions that will make me happy, fulfilled, and entertained in the here and now. So, I'm focusing a lot on that. When I was younger, I had concepts of finding my purpose. Did I see it in my future at the time that I would become a nurse and soon-to-be a physician? Were these things ever a part of my plan? That's something that we're all taught to envision. And so, before I nailed that down, I found myself interested in diseases, health, and medicine.

I would spend time on my own looking at videos and books about obscure diseases, and I was so drawn to them. I thought they were so interesting. I wanted to know what the symptoms were and how the person was feeling. So, I didn't necessarily think, *Oh, I'm going to be a doctor or a nurse.* That was the first inkling I wanted to go in the direction of health and medicine.

I did not have much exposure to physicians as a child. I didn't know any personally. I went to college knowing I was interested in health and medicine and a little about the nursing profession; So, I decided I would be a nurse. That was not a career I knew much about, but I did have exposure to some family members who were nurses. After learning a little bit more about it, I was thinking, *Okay, I want to do that.* I felt good about it. I thought, *Great, I'm interested in this stuff.* I know the process to get there, so it was intentional. But I still had an inkling in my mind, that maybe I was interested in being a doctor. Still, I needed to learn more about it.

I thought medicine was just for people with opportunities, resources, and finances. I don't have all those things, so that may not be for me. As I started working as a nurse and gaining more experience in the day-to-day life of a nurse, specifically once I got into the Neonatal Intensive Care Unit (NICU), which at the time I was still in college before I even got my nursing license, I got to have a NICU experience. It was cool, and I love the science of babies and their illnesses in the intensive care unit and how that differs so much from adult care.

Then, I started to see what the physician does, and that notion I had in my mind grew and developed. But I was already on track to being a nurse, right? I was not going to give up on that. I pursued it heavily and went straight into NICU directly out of college. Even though people told me I should do medical surgical nursing before trying to do a specialty, that wasn't what I wanted to do. I responded with, "I know what I want. I like this and don't see the point in wasting time doing something else just because people tell me that's the better way." Yes, I believe in mentorship, but when your heart tells you your purpose is in one direction, you should follow that. I ignored that advice and went straight into Neonatal Nursing with no regrets. I loved it there. This was the type of nursing I was meant to be doing.

However, the inkling that I put in the back of my mind just continued to grow more and more. I was now working independently as a nurse, having a good time and learning all types of different skills, and getting over my fears of having someone's life living in my hands daily. I was still getting more and more interested in the role of a physician. But then I was at a crossroad reflecting on my life, *you have a career, and you have done all that work; you went to nursing school. Why would you give that up? Why would you change when you know people would look at you and say,* "You have a great life, you have a great job, you enjoy it, and you work with fun people? It would be crazy to give up to pursue this other thing and start over."

Collision With My Purpose

The deciding factor for me, the more I looked into it and found out what path to choose from, was when my dad had a heart attack. When he left the hospital, he had hundreds of dollars in medication that had to be filled every three months. At the time, he was not working, and there were no resources given to us at discharge; they gave us one little coupon as if to say, *Oh, use this, and it'll take a couple of dollars off.* But to expect someone to pay $400 dollars or more for medication every one to two months is entirely unreasonable. Especially if you know that person doesn't have insurance and they are not working, or whatever other barriers they may have. That isn't feasible.

This left me in a tizzy when he left the hospital. How will I fix this? How will I navigate this for someone who can't do it for themselves? Three months later, my dad had to go back to the hospital because of that heart attack. Here we are again at the starting point. It was like, what are we going to do about this and blah, blah, blah. This time, he ended up going to a different facility, Grady Hospital, which many people know in Atlanta. It caters to a low-income population—people who do not have insurance, undocumented people, and a lot of minorities who need medication and medical care. Grady is saving lives regularly.

I talked to my father's physician and told him, "Listen, this is our situation; I need something. I need resources, social work assistance, and something to help him move forward so that he can afford this medication and we can plan for cardiac rehab, etc. What are you going to do about it?"

"We're going to figure this out. I'm going to do research," he said. "I am going to find out if he has to take this $400-a-month medication. And whether it is any more effective than other medications for a population—you know, for older adults in their fifties and sixties, a black male, etc.? If I don't find anything like that, we can change it. We can make it something different. We can work with you wherever you are."

That doctor was amazing. Long story short, when my father left the hospital, and after all the discussions with his doctor, he only had seventy dollars' worth of medication. Medications that were $400 came down to twenty dollars because of that doctor and the work and effort he was willing to put in to give individualized medical care rather than blanket care.

That was like the nail in the coffin for me. I was like, this is what I want to be doing. I want to be making that type of difference in patients' lives. So, after that, I immediately said, "I'm applying to medical school and taking all the projects and the curriculum. That's what I want to be doing. This happened for a reason." I felt so driven and alive. It meant something. Within that scenario, I experienced a collision with my purpose; that is what brought me to where I am today.

My Values and Beliefs

Reflecting on the fact that the current society we are living in is innately unfair and prejudiced. It is filled with all sorts of injustices that are intentionally put in place to create oppression and prejudices which gradually infiltrate into people's minds. As it relates to my values and beliefs and my purpose, I believe the same intent that those systems are working to create these problems is the same determination you need to have in breaking them down because you don't just sort of fall upon better times. You must create them and be forceful and deliberate about making them happen. How that manifest in my life is this belief that society is unfair, and some systems are in place that are working against me drives me to join various causes.

In my medical school right now, I am one of the three-course liaisons for my class. And our job is to ask questions like, What are the problems with the curriculum? What are the things that we need to add or the things that we need to take away? I am intentional about what the future generation needs to learn and understand. I speak out about any of those things that I feel needs to be included in those gaps in minority medicine.

I must address the various communities I serve in fulfilling and pursuing my purpose. I fit in the community of being a woman, a black woman, a member of the health care group, and my family; these are the communities I fit into. There are many ways that I'm contributing to those other things. The family ones are more obvious to pin down, and many of us share. When it comes to my community in the healthcare field, the contributions I'm making motivated me to become a doctor in the first place. Physicians' power and influence are very different from nurses in that they can make administration changes with policies and finance, while others can't. That motivated me to want to become a physician.

I saw there were not enough black women, black people, minorities, and biopic individuals in medicine. Who will do the work to fill those gaps, if not the people most closely affected by those gaps? This is part of the contributions I want to make in medicine, to fill those gaps. My existence in the room is important because I already contribute to the conversations. People who are on the road to being physicians that are the opposite of me, such as white males, could never imagine or think about the perspective that I am providing to them when we are in these rooms together, whether it's about the patient, policy, and law. When it comes to health care and medicine, they don't think about those things. It's my position and purpose to be in those rooms and say, "Hey, you guys didn't know about this, but here is this issue that people of color are facing, and here's why if you look at research articles, they will show you what I'm talking about."

I can be the Knight in those scenarios, be a part of that chess board to make those changes to get to the end goal. I am making contributions in that way. I'm one of two in my class doing health disparities electives. Unsurprisingly, the only two people doing the health disparities elective are the two black people.

Recently I attended a showing of the documentary, *Aftershock*, which is about black maternal mortality and morbidity, how black women are dying at astonishing rates when it comes to childbirth in the U.S., and how we have a horrible mortality rate compared to other developed countries. The Black Mothers Matter organization in New York is into lobbying and changing cultures within hospitals so that we can have less black female mortality. The documentary moved me and touched me. It was great to be in a room of black physicians, black nurses, and black moms, and just being together knowing that we're working for this one goal.

Now, I'm trying to nudge the preceptor, the licensed clinician who supervises nursing students, regarding my elective; she is one of the curriculum team heads. I am discussing with her about how I can get that documentary added to our curriculum on reproduction. It would be the perfect movie to add to our health systems class or a two-hour course about morals and ethics in medicine. Since she is the preceptor, it's an excellent opportunity to present the documentary to her. I was thinking, *If that happens, Danielle, that's a battle.* That battle would have only existed once you tried to implement it. Saying these things are happening one at a time, celebrating them, and being happy about them is all cumulative and will get you to the goal you're looking for.

Aligning With Purpose

Aligning yourself with purpose is accepting the trials you face, and saying to yourself, I know this is the path that will lead me to where I want to go. I'm scared, and those things challenge me, but it means I'm choosing that difficult path because that's what walking on purpose feels like. It's coming to those mountains and those obstacles head-on saying, "I know what I'm getting into, it's worth it, and I'm willing." That's aligning yourself with your purpose.

The first step to take is doing some introspective work in finding my purpose, asking myself what is important to me, what drives me, and what I place value in. We often have so many outside influences telling us what we think is important; sometimes, when you do some soul-searching, you realize that thing isn't very important. It may be important to my parents, friends, and coworkers, but not to me. It is hard to decipher those types of wants and whether they come from you or an outside influence.

When you conduct your self-analysis, maybe what you thought was your plan and your purpose wasn't. It's being okay with that and accepting life comes in stages. Then, acknowledge, that's what I thought my purpose was, but I'm willing to move onto another stage and change the picture of what I thought the future would be. Being open to change and following those opportunities is another way to find your purpose and keep your ears open.

There is a psychology framework that says change only happens once you get to a certain level of frustration. Being annoyed isn't enough, and bored is not enough. You must get to the point of total frustration before deciding to change. That's all a part of finding your purpose.

What drives this sensation? What would it look like if something were to change? Would that get rid of that feeling? Those types of insights—identifying the frustration, identifying what's inside you that motivates you, that pushes you, and being open to change, if it were to come along, I think, are all ways that can lead to your purpose.

Discussion About Purpose

In my generation and circle of friends and family, speaking about purpose is common. We have a lot of discussions about purpose, what it means, and conversations about success, what success looks like, and what we value in success. It's the twenties, thirties era, which is a big time to talk about purpose. You set your future with what you will do for the next twenty or thirty years. You must make many big decisions based on your purpose during this time. I'm grateful I have found that at my current stage in life what that looks like for me,

In contrast, people have many other careers, purposes, and passions but don't have an obvious way to get there. I have a lot of friends in that place right now, in their late twenties and early thirties, and I encourage them in their decisions and help them find the resources that will answer some of their questions.

My Legacy

How will I be remembered in this life? I'm very in the moment. Anyone, including family, will remember me; I wouldn't say I live my life thinking, "Oh, I hope people remember this about me, or that I did this or that. What are people going to think about me? They're not going to at all. And I'm okay with that. What will make me feel good are the decisions I've made in my life? That's more what I think about.

For example, sixty years from now, will I make the right decisions for myself, my family, and others before I die? I hope that level of peace is what I have when I look back on my life. The idea that the purpose you feel you have had generational effects is something that I buy into. I may not know the names of the people who created this space and opportunity for me, but I'm thankful to them for that work. I hope to be included in that category after I'm gone.

Mentorship

So many people have pushed and encouraged me, giving me advice and information I didn't have before, even people who didn't know anything about what I was pursuing, like you, Dr. Stephenson. Regardless of their mentorship and belief that I could do this thing I want to pursue, I know I have the skills, the trade, and the ambition to make those things happen, which is the foundation that I need for that social support. These people believe in me; because of them, I can push hard and harder. It's so important. As for the specific stepping stones to pursuing a particular career or purpose, I cannot stress the importance of mentorship in laying out what those steps are.

Even though the steps may be obvious, lay them out. Have a timeline for each objective, indicating when it needs to get done. I had no idea how to do this. It took other mentors who came before me and said, "Hey, I know this information, and it will help you get to where you're going." I think about those things for myself, leading me to all this unsolicited advice I give, but it's so important. I always find ways to mentor people, whether in a structured, formal way, or just with people I meet in my everyday life.

I am in an Envision Scholars program at my school to get high school students interested in STEM, an acronym for Science, Technology, Engineering, and Math; and also encourage their interest in medicine. It also allows me to mentor them. I told everybody pursuing pre-med about my freshman year and how I had to drop my chemistry class. I was going to fail. I have a "W" on my transcript, meaning I withdrew and couldn't cut it to the end of that class. It's important to communicate your failures to people so they know just because it happened doesn't mean you won't get to where you want to go.

Takeaway

Refrain from listening to people telling you that you must be a perfect cookie cutter to achieve your dream. It's important to remember that there's no age limit to mentorship. At the end of life, at the beginning of life, learn something from someone else and be able to give advice. You can pursue everything you have ever been interested in. If you want to change or change a career, there is always time to do that. It is always okay to start looking at doing that introspection and looking at your relationships and having that self-engagement to find a purpose later in life.

I want to impart to people to always be open to finding a new or original purpose at any stage of their life. I think that can be true, but I also believe it doesn't have to be that black and white; it doesn't have to be wrapped like a neat bow. That overarching purpose may not connect in any way, but it matters to you. Honoring it and saying it's okay for me to do this and that at the same time, or at different stages of my life is equally valuable as having that one overarching purpose that can guide your whole life.

Miracle After Miracle

"Keep your hope. Keep trusting, open your eyes, and follow God. He is a faithful God. He is a perfect Father. He will always guide you."

Susana Somawidjaja

Susana is a wife, mother of two children, and a woman of God. She is the founder and owner of Agape Montessori Home School for children ages zero to four years old. Susana deeply connects with children and advocates for their education, safety, and well-being.

My Early Years

I was born and raised in Indonesia. My family worshiped Buddhism, but they sent me to a Christian school. Eventually, I started reading the Bible in third grade and fell in love with Jesus. I truly sought him, and I dedicated my life to him when I was at an early age.

The Importance of Purpose

Purpose is why something exists, probably why someone exists. It's like a divine big picture. Knowing what we are created for and why helps us navigate our lives to value life. We can use our time here wisely and point out, not only to ourselves but to people around us, what our purpose is so we can leave a good legacy for them. Since finding my purpose, I had a special divine moment when I met God that changed my perspective on why I'm here on this Earth.

My Purpose

My purpose is to glorify God and enjoy my walk with him, with the talent and whatever he has already poured into me. I found my purpose. I have been going through all of my life stages, and I know God called me for this. I want to make a difference in the lives of children. From 0—5 years old are crucial ages when children accept and absorb everything at the beginning of their early years. I want to impart true love. I want to impart whatever I can to children, so they have an excellent foundation to grow, and their life can also impact their families.

I didn't have a good childhood. I have lived with several different families, moving from house to house. Now, I realize that I did not feel loved at that time. I missed the love from my father. Then when I met God, I found the Father's love that changed my life. Jesus is my Father. Since that moment, I have had a special relationship with him. Everybody around me told me to have a purposeful life. I need to be valuable; I need to be useful when I grow up. In my heart, I know that Jesus is my God. I am just going to follow him. I am dedicating my life to him, to serve him.

My husband and I came to the United States (U.S.) in 1998, when I was only twenty-five years old. We came here because of the large riots in Indonesia. A few years later, in July 2000, I gave birth to my daughter, Madeline. In 2002, she was diagnosed with a terminal disease called Spinal Muscular Atrophy, type II (SMA type 2). We were told that she would not live past two years old. I was a stay-at-home mom because of her situation. I did not speak English well, because remember I was raised in Indonesia. I tried my best to learn about the different medical terminology to communicate with medical doctors and therapists for my daughter.

Our daughter Madeline's terminal diagnosis was our turning point. My husband decided to give his life to God, and we both got baptized. From that moment, God was real for our family. We experienced how the Lord worked many miracles in our daughter's life. My husband and I started serving God in our church. My first ministry was a children's ministry. I was twenty-seven years old, which was twenty years ago. That was my first ministry until now. I saw how God was working in every area of our lives. Miracle after miracle happened until Madeline was twenty-two years old.

Why Agape Montessori Home School

When my daughter turned eighteen, she decided to live outside our house. She lived in the dorm after she got accepted at Georgia State University. Before that, I had lived my life entirely for her. I stayed at home and took care of her and our son, Brighton, who is now eighteen years old.

Conversely, I love people and needed to go out and meet people. Back in my country, I have a bachelor's degree, although I never used my degree. But I wanted to work outside our home. I was like, I don't care what it is; I just want to work. So, I got three jobs. I worked in a restaurant at night for quick money. Working in the restaurant helped me to meet people, so I felt energized. This was when I decided to find a job where I could fully use my skills. I got a job at PetSmart because I have two dogs, and I was a cashier and worked overnight in a factory.

One day, a lady approached me and asked, "Hey, do you know anybody who loves children and wants to work at a school?" She specifically requested an Asian lady. "I love kids, and I love to teach kids," I said. I told her I served in the children's ministry at church, so she When I graduated from school in August, I felt proud that I had my degree and knowledge. So, I started putting everything together from whatever I had in my house. When COVID hit, many daycares closed, so parents working at home had a problem because they could not get anything done because of the distractions their children caused. Having toddlers in their homes was stressful, and they didn't know how to handle them, work simultaneously, and run errands. They stressed over COVID.

Invited me over to the school, which is the school where I was working before I opened my own school. That was the first time I had experienced a Montessori environment. It slowly opened my eyes. This is a friendly environment for a preschool; it's not a daycare. They told me they wanted me to attend school to get my diploma, and I agreed.

I found a school in Arizona, and when I was almost finished, the school closed. So, I completed my diploma online because it was in a different time zone than where I lived. During my classes, I was so tired. Sometimes, I would fall asleep because it was so late. I was usually finishing my classwork very late, between midnight and 2:00 a.m. And then, suddenly, God gave me a verse that inspired me, and I began drawing because it kept me awake. When I do something with my hands, God gives me a verse like 1 Corinthians 13. This chapter is about love. Thank God I was able to handle the situations around me, and I got to find out what true love is.

So, I started to open my home to provide childcare. I asked if anybody wanted to bring their children to my house so I could help them out, and I would also be able to practice my skills at the same time. One of my friends from my church asked me to babysit their son. At that time, I only had one kid. So, I started with two kids in October 2020. Then, I met Dr. Stephenson's grandson, Kanaan, when working at my previous school. So, he enrolled him in my childcare, too. I love what I'm doing, and I follow wherever God leads me.

I soon found I was constantly babysitting everybody's kids. I looked forward to it daily because these children gave me energy, and I wanted to pour more into them. Every child is different. Whenever I see they are flourishing, that's like my reward.

It doesn't matter whose child comes in my house, they will receive Agape, which means unconditional love—because that's how they grow. God gives me words at the beginning of the year. He gave me the word, Agape, in 2021; it was a breakthrough. From that point, God gave me the school's name during my training and the vision for the school. The name of my school is Agape Montessori Home School. I started with one child. Then, by the beginning of 2021, we had five students. Now, we have fourteen in total and are at full capacity with a staff of four. Many people have heard about us through their friends or family. God said we would be growing, and we have. We will probably need to move from my home to a larger building, but I am still determining when that will be.

Do Not Lose Hope

Do not lose hope because you may feel stuck in your journey. Sometimes we think we are in a deep valley, in a dark place, and don't know where to go. But keep your hope. Keep trusting, open your eyes, and follow God. He is a faithful God. He is a perfect Father. He will always guide you. I don't have a father figure, but I have the real Father. So, seek him, seek him. Jesus is everything. And when you finally have that relationship with him, you will hear his voice, and he will show you the way.

Even though you may be in the dark, he will never leave and forsake you, so do not lose hope. I am a Christian not because of religion, but I am a Christian because I have a relationship with God. So basically, never stop communicating with God, do it daily. Honestly, I cannot do anything without him. I am still amazed at how God leads me.

I came from a country where we do not speak English, and now I am a teacher here in the United States. But I need to figure out why. For example, when one child throws a tantrum and nobody knows what happened or why the child is upset, nobody can handle it. However, when I pursue this child, they will come and sit with me, and then settle in God's presence. I can make a significant difference with everything that purpose already has set in my life, my family, and community. For now, I am praying that I can reach more people in real need—those in need who cannot afford what we have.

Impacted by My Purpose

The real thing that I see right now is change. You know, the children that I serve, they are flourishing. Sometimes they influence their family. I can help minister to their parents as well. If they get frustrated, I am here to help and assist them. When they see the difference in their loved one, they feel confident they know their child has a bright future. What I'm doing right now is not only teaching the little ones, but also ministering to the parents so they can share with other people.

I have energy to pursue my purpose, because I know that I am glorifying God and enjoying it with him. I never feel empty because I know where I get the source of my strength. I know some people think, *How can you do this?* I know it's tiring, but I'm happy. I'm enjoying it because I know I am called to do this. God has equipped me for this, and whenever I need help, he will send the right people at the right time. It is incredible how things work when you are walking with him.

I Walk in My Purpose

Walking in purpose means that when you go through your journey, you follow Him—walk, and keep moving forward. When you have the path already set and stay on it, you have someone who can align with it, so you don't go wrong. You are not stuck walking around the place. You're moving forward. But to move forward, you need to know where and who you are going with.

Walking in my purpose means walking intentionally and finally reaching my purpose. You need to have a pure heart and intention in a relationship. You built communication; you built relationships. So, when you do something intentionally, you are doing it wholeheartedly; you're willing to put in your energy, time, and intention. You must be determined to spend your life with whomever God trusts you with.

Discussion About Purpose in My Circle

Purpose is a topic for discussion in my family and circle of friends. As a matter of fact, in our church, we also have this conversation a lot because you have to set your vision right. And then from there, you will also write down: What is your purpose? Are you going to find your purpose? Going through this process, you realize that if you have a vision, you will find your goal.

How to Find Purpose

My suggestion to find purpose is don't waste time, value your life, whatever you have, because God created you for a purpose. God created you for a special purpose on this Earth. So, you are able to glorify him in everything you do. Don't waste your time, stress, or get depressed. But when you find your purpose, and you are focused on that, you can see the value of your own life.

My Legacy

So, whenever I leave this Earth, I want you all to know I want to be remembered as a woman of faith. That's what I want everyone to remember. Because whatever I go through, faith is the key.

At one point in my life, I was lost, and everybody around me called me useless. During that time, what I heard going through my mind gave me depression. Why did I need to be born if I'm useless? I know that sometimes I feel like everybody around me doesn't love me. They despise me. They make me look like a bad person that cannot do anything. But then the word of God came to me in Jeremiah 29:11, *The plan is for my hope and future.* So when I read that verse, my plan for you is for your hope and future, it keeps me going. I do not have to pay attention to what people say, but I must listen to what my Father says. Please put your trust in him. He never fails.

My Final Word

I realize I still have a great purpose I need to achieve. This conversation has been an eye-opener. There is a lot of stuff out there to make a legacy in our life and a difference in the people around us. And wherever I go, I will share this testimony. And it's true. It is not because of me. It is my life, my journey. I am nothing without God; that is my life, and I want everybody to have that experience too.

Hurt People Hurt Other People

"Hurt people hurt other people. Forgive and heal."

Ashley Bischoff

A shley Bischoff is a mother of two wonderful daughters. She's an Information Technology (I.T.) support manager, Health Care Administrator, and founder of Light House Hope Services, a nonprofit organization. She lives a peaceful life where she takes a yearly self-awareness sabbatical. Whether it is a solo vacation or investment in a holistic approach to living a more profound life to unplug, her goal is to cleanse with a focus on intentionally reconnecting with God and the universe embodied within.

My Early Years

My childhood was enveloped with Faith, Empathy, Kindness, Helping, Family, Peace, and Spirituality. Growing up in a large southern Christian family with nine siblings, my mother instilled in us to always love one another. Our home was our sanctuary, a place of peace and love. We were constantly reminded that everyone is a child of God and to remember what God proclaims about us; no one is above the other.

At an early age, we were taught that we all have a unique gift with our blessings. Also, we were reminded that none of us are immune to hardship. When we experience hardship, we must thank the lord for the opportunity to learn and grow.

Use everything you encounter in life, good or bad, to move on to the process of growing. Nothing is considered bad when you use the experience to grow and seek to find positivity in the situation. We were also taught to have empathy. When you see someone in need, and you are privileged enough to have the means to help, extend support to those in need; for you will one day require guidance from someone with the means, knowledge, and values that can catapult you to the next level in this life's journey.

Broad Definition of Purpose

We should have a good understanding of our Purpose. Purpose can carry many definitions, and a simple explanation of Purpose is living with the intent of why God formed us in our mother's womb. The Purpose is the reason we are here to live in the intentions of God. My Purpose was a journey for me. It has taken time to think about and search the universe, listen, and determine my Purpose. So, we must know what our Purpose is. Knowing our Purpose will bring ease and peace to our lives.

What Is My Purpose?

Purpose is a dynamic and multi-layered aspect of life, continually evolving with each life stage. As a mother to two daughters, my role and Purpose in their lives have shifted over time. I recognize that my commitment to them is ongoing and will never be fully realized; it's a path of perpetual growth and understanding. My dedication extends not only to my daughters but also to their future generations. It's crucial to acknowledge the legacy we're creating for our descendants. Ultimately, Purpose is about living a life true to one's calling, which can have many meanings.

My life's Purpose is dynamic and multifaceted, evolving through different stages. My foremost role is as a mother, which encompasses being an educator and a role model for my children. My goal is to guide them into adulthood, adapting my approach to suit each stage of their development. In this journey, I serve as one of their primary windows to the wider world.

My Purpose for my children continues. However, I must learn to pivot with each stage of my life. Having the ability and discernment to pivot will allow them the opportunity to discover their Purpose and move forward to determine and understand the Purpose in their lives. What do I mean by multifaceted? I still must maintain my commitment to myself and the world in which I live. At this stage in my life, the children are grown. Now, my primary focus is on how I give back to this universe, which has been so gracious to me.

I have developed a nonprofit organization called LightHouse Hope Services that provides support to individuals who are in domestic abuse situations. We guide and assist people in those circumstances. Our desire is to eradicate domestic abuse, and if we can eliminate it in one person, that would be a great benefit for us and a great benefit for them.

Love God and love people. And that is the primary Purpose for all of us to love our fellow sisters and brothers that we interact with daily.

Purpose in My Family and Circle of Friends

Purpose has become a common topic. It was inflicted upon us because of what we experienced in the last two years—COVID, the George Floyd situation, and all of us experiencing the unveiling of racism. These events caused many of us to focus on our Purpose. It made me recall an experience I had walking on the beach. I noticed several people intently looking for and gathering the perfect shell to give as a gift or display in their homes, etc. And right as I looked down, I saw the sun glistening on a broken shell. Even though it was broken, there was still a perfect spot on that shell that shined. So, I started searching for the broken shells with a beautiful spot worth giving as a gift or displaying in my home. I gave several friends and family members those shells. I shared my experience and asked them to remember the broken pieces in their lives and those of the people around them and know that we are all still beautiful in our brokenness.

I continue my purpose journey to determine how to serve someone in need. I pose these questions to myself; How can I be a good example to everybody that I meet daily? Or how can I be a beacon of hope to someone not knowing what they are going through? So, yes, it is a big topic. And a big journey for many people.

How To Discover Purpose

Live in the present moment. If you don't know your Purpose, are you living in the present? Are you present in your life? Or are you just going to a job every day, working 9:00 to 5:00, and doing the same thing again, feeling unfulfilled? We must take time to meditate, engage in the universe, and understand and know what our Purpose is.

I Am Aligned With My Purpose

It goes back to joy! When you are in alignment, you have peace and don't mind sharing because you have no fear. There is enough for all of us. You want to provide guidance where guidance is needed for the advancement and production of others. You get the opportunity to experience joy, to see that you have contributed to the success of others. Aligning with your Purpose is essential because if we don't, we withhold the benefits of those in need and withhold benefits from ourselves from experiencing the joy of helping someone. When you are not in alignment, you always feel like you are searching for yourself. Something needs to be added, but I must know what it is. It is like emptiness. When you find your Purpose, that void is filled. Once I discovered my Purpose and understood what that is, I got the privilege of having fulfillment and joy in my life.

My Values Are My Faith, Empathy, and Kindness

I believe in embracing my faith, empathy, and kindness. I think those are important values aimed at helping others. And having that desire for family and peace for the family as we seek our Purpose. I grew up in a very peaceful household, and that's what I would like to provide for someone else and, of course, for the spirituality of your soul and living in peace.

I Discovered My Purpose Through a Traumatic Event

I had my Collision with my Purpose during a traumatic event in my life. Some may consider it crushing, but you must crush grapes to make fine wine. We may encounter crushing situations in our lives that we may consider devastating, but instead of thinking you did something wrong, or you are bitter that this happened, or that life sucks, use the experience positively. If you continue being resentful or have hatred, you prolong your healing and forfeit your blessings. Let it go and use it for the betterment of others and yourself. That will serve us as individuals and our communities much better; that's something to pay attention to. Your Purpose also centers you. If you are centered, focused, and aligned with your Purpose, you have a direction in which to go.

Purpose in Our Classrooms

A course about finding your Purpose should be taught in our schools. Growing up in Louisiana, we learned that blinders on horses guided them and kept them focused on one area. Teaching purpose at an early age would help students in schools to focus on their Purpose, and things outside the blinders, such as bullying, what you wear, etc., will not be in view. It is something that should be promoted in our schools.

What Informs My Purpose

My nonprofit organization provides aid and guidance to those in domestic abuse situations. When I was in an abusive relationship, I always found solace and peace occasionally when I went to a hotel for rest. It became common for me to feel and know when my body and mind required peace. When I went to the hotel, I could get at least one night where I would feel safe and peaceful. That occasional peace and rest gave me the courage to take the opportunity to leave that environment permanently. So that is a service we provide; to give peace to someone so they can build the courage to leave their abusive situation permanently. We don't think about how domestic violence impacts the abused, family members, the workplace, and its lasting effect on everyone, even the abuser.

On social media, I saw a video of a person being thrown across the room into an entertainment center! The abuser does not consider the danger and death they could cause the abused. Seeing this video made me ask, "Is this still happening?" Someone needs to do something. My next thought was: *You are someone!* I think it goes back to using your trauma for the betterment of others. I believe it is my innate ability to help someone in need if I have the means. God knows us. The hairs on our heads are numbered. Therefore, the abusive situation I was exposed to was for me to help as many as possible to get the courage to leave their situation and grow from their encounter. It is encouraging for me and for everyone that I support to be able to help them on their life's journey.

My Purpose as A Health Care Administrator

As patients, you receive a manual of benefits awarded to you. However, most of us need to take the time to understand them so we can obtain the full benefits of our policy. As healthcare administrators, we help you understand the full benefits of your insurance. What we do is help you gain the full benefit of the policy that works for you. We assist you in maximizing the potential of the policy you choose by ensuring that you receive all the benefits available to you.

We need that type of support and information to give us a better understanding of what these products are. My partner and I are working towards better legislation as well. That is one of our long-term goals because insurance has changed dramatically over the years, as we all know. Here is one example of how much it has changed: I had my daughters 2 1/2 years apart. The co-pay for my first daughter was $15–$20. After the birth of my second daughter, we received an itemized bill for about $7,000. WOW! What changed, and why did it change? We are still paying the same premiums. It was a methodical change. The lab work, radiology, injections, etc., are documented and charged. Yet, there are still questions as to why a physician must consult an insurance agent before service is provided. I understand some changes were needed in this area, but some illnesses are being scrutinized, and lives are lost due to this policy. However, there are always case-by-case situations.

I Want to Be Remembered

I want to be remembered as someone who loved God and his people and was empathetic and kind. I hope people see me as someone who understands and knows we all have a story, and as a person who understands and lives in the truth that we should all be treated with kindness because we are not privy to each other's personal history. A person who understood that the unfortunate events that I experienced were because the person inflicting it was dealing with unrecognized or unhealed trauma themselves. Hurt people hurt other people. Forgive and heal.

Takeaway For the Reader

The reader should take the time for themselves and invest in themselves because finding your Purpose is a huge investment in yourself and everyone around you and your communities. Take the time to meditate, learn what your Purpose is, and at the same time, explore the benefits of what your Purpose can yield. There are many benefits to knowing your Purpose. The value of the sense of peace is immeasurable. When you help someone, think about the old cliché, *It is better to give than to receive.* It is a blessing to give and a gift you give yourself when you give to others.

I would say take the time, meditate, whatever it is that you do, whatever or whoever you consider your God to be, whatever you consider as time for yourself—take that time. Spend time with yourself in your universe and listen. If you listen, God will speak to you, and it is up to you to grasp that discernment and understand your Purpose. Always remember *attitude and gratitude are everything.*

Being intentional brings focus to what matters. When you have that uneasiness about yourself, be deliberate in determining and exploring what that is, whatever it takes. Give yourself that gift, invest in yourself, and discover what it is. Be purposeful and figure out what that uneasiness is in your mind, body, and spirit. Focus on what is causing those restless nights or causing you to daydream and your mind to be wandering. Be intentional on getting to the bottom of what is happening? Why am I feeling this way? Share your gift. We all have a gift and withholding that would be a disservice to you and the person in need. That is not something any of us want to do. If we can provide a service to someone else or provide anything to someone, we would be glad to provide it. So, let us all be conscientious and focus on finding out what our gifts are and what you have that someone else can benefit from. Being intentional would provide you with that ease and relieve someone who may need what you have to offer. It will bring immense joy and make the world a better place. If we are not all happy, it affects us all. We are all connected in some way or another.

I want to reiterate, take the time for yourself. Make time for yourself! If we remember 9/11, we all felt united. For a moment, color and financial status did not matter. I would venture to say nothing mattered except humanity. During that time, we felt connected about as strongly as some of us may have felt the disconnection during the

George Floyd incident and the unveiling of racism. Let us get that correlation of love and relationships back and do our part to understand our Purpose. This would guide us to know and understand that we are all one. I suggest rushing to understand our Purpose rather than rushing to judgment. Because the life around us could change at any moment, make the time, make each day count, live life to its fullest, and appreciate everyone around you.

From Devastation To Finding My Purpose

"Please, get me through this. I want to get through this.
I cannot believe this is happening to me," I said,
as I bathed myself in sage.

Añya Grant

Añya is a boss marketer for a digital firm and a heart healer. She helps women and families look and feel younger without giving up carbs or working out. She helps them gain the courage to take the next step to do whatever their heart desires.

My Early Years

In my early years, I did not trust myself, ultimately not trusting and listening to my inner voice. I was super fearful of everything, especially of getting accepted into college or the university. I was afraid of any little thing that was outside of my comfort zone. So anything, like starting a new job or opening a new bank account, scared me. I had to develop the courage to get into uncomfortable situations and continue to challenge myself and trust that the outcome was going to bring me closer to where I needed to be.

It took years to surrender and appreciate that, even right now, in this stage of my life, where I am dating and trying to have the expectation of finding the right partner, that fear brings me back to my old ways of thinking like, *Oh my God, I'm so afraid! I don't want to put myself out there! I don't want to talk to anybody!* I have to constantly remind myself to slow down, take a breath, and know that what is coming to me will come to me.

I grew up in Jamaica with my grandmother and aunt. When I was twelve, I moved to Canada to live with my father and his wife, who I now call my second mom. The change was traumatic—moving from a nontraditional family where grandma and my aunt took care of me, to living with my parents and trying to develop a relationship with them, as well as my biological mom. It was during this difficult transition that I got to know who I am. Within the new family dynamics, I was able to find joy, and was able to release my anger and anxiety that I had as a child. I also overcame the shock of moving to a country with four seasons and different cultural values. I was determined to make it through because I didn't know any other way.

My parents were very supportive even though there was friction between my mother and father. There were many disagreements about how I should be raised. But, if I had to do it again, with the wisdom I have gathered, I would school my parents on how to take care of me properly. Regardless, my childhood was beautiful. I took music classes, and my grandmother ensured I did the best activities. I participated in dancing, singing, and poetry. I loved the arts, so when I moved to Canada, the one thing that stuck with me and carried me through the many different dynamics of life was the art form. I fell in love with dance, music, and culture, which kept me grounded in who I became.

It's the Vibrancy

When I stop and reflect on the woman I am today, I still have my culture and can bring it out at will. I keep myself young and vibrant. Everything that I do must be fun and include playfulness. That is how I keep going through painful and good times. And now it's just part of who I am!

What is Purpose?

Purpose is like a light within that motivates an individual to wake up and choose life. Our journey is filled with many ups and downs and twists and turns. If I did not have a purpose when I woke up and was grateful to carry on that mission every day, I would allow these little things to bog me down. So, purpose is this light that keeps us alive? Purpose keeps an individual on the path to choose life no matter the condition.

Why is Understanding Purpose Important?

There might be someone who is still determining what their purpose is. It's important to keep seeking your purpose in this life, even if you are at the point where you don't know what it is. You may have to ask yourself, "Can I take this course to figure it out? Can I read this book to figure it out?" Until you know what your purpose is, constantly strive to figure it out. It is a driving force. And what is more important than actually knowing today, right now, what your purpose is? It is your pursuit of purpose.

My Purpose

My current purpose is to help small business owners maximize and impact as many people as possible by creating a marketing strategy for them and helping them build out those strategies with an amazing marketing team. I get joy and fulfillment when I can see the impact my clients are making on their own families, hundreds of families, thousands of families, and different people's lives. Many lives have shifted financially; a lot of lives had to be shifted purposely. Many people have become very driven towards defining their purpose based on the services my clients have received.

My other purpose is to help families by focusing on the matriarch of the family unit, by assisting that woman in feeling younger and vibrant so that she can open up her heart to create the life she desires. Because of a woman's magnitude and power, as she becomes more in tune with who she is, what she's doing, and the intention behind it, it impacts the rest of the family unit.

In my own life there were little clues that I was unhappy or never satisfied wherever I decided to live. I've constantly searched for a home. I went to Brazil after college and fell in love with the culture. I lived there for a year and said, "Okay, this is home." I had all these plans to stay in Brazil permanently, have a family, and live in a nice house on the beach. In the midst of my planning, I was robbed in broad daylight and was devastated. Suddenly, I was living in a crummy place I hated, with no windows; it was super dark. At the time, I was also doing marketing but couldn't work. So, I wasn't living like I had envisioned in this Brazilian country.

One day, I remember walking on the beach, trying to shift my energy. I was thinking, *What could happen next?* I was robbed *again* in broad daylight the following week. So, I concluded that I would never ask that question again. Things could get worse. I decided to mellow out and take it all in, so I would never forget it. I wrote in my journal that night and asked, *How long will this last? When is it going to get brighter again? What's coming towards me? What's the next chapter of life, Añya? Do you know what will put a smile on your face again?* I asked myself those questions and then decided to return to Canada, although it no longer felt like home.

I also considered the possibility of moving to New York, where my biological mother lived. For so long, I had believed that home is a place within a specific location. However, I had to learn that the home I have been searching for is within me. Home can be anywhere when it starts with you. I had to realize that by doing the same thing repeatedly, trying to move to different places, the only thing you take with you is yourself. Once you find a home within you, you can make one wherever you go. I embody that and enjoy the beauty and simplicity of life.

There's a morning ritual that I have developed for myself that sets the tone for my day. It consists of writing a mantra down, putting it on my walls, and chanting for about 5–10 minutes. I repeat that mantra, and then I am ready for the day. If I want an extra oomph, I journal about some things on my mind, some frustrating things, and release that to paper. And then I might chant a little bit more. So when I talk about being a heart healer, I help women determine what makes them happy and how we can ensure that it is incorporated into their daily life.

I've been tiptoeing around the hearts of men a little less because I have been married before and have been in a very mission-focused relationship. Without speaking on it too much, it was a marriage that tugged at emotions and had many unresolved childhood traumas that bonded us. As a woman, I did the best that I knew how to support my husband and assist him until he could get to that place of self-realization. Although I still need to gain experience working with men and their heart issues, I have the compassion to help them feel accepted and feel the nurturing that many men desire.

What Informs My Purpose

I lost my husband in a car accident. He passed away suddenly, and fourteen hours later when I figured out what happened, my world had changed tremendously. At the time, I was devastated. I couldn't focus and even forgot who I was. But now, I can say it was for the better, because I always want to see the blessings in everything.

After losing my husband, I didn't know what direction to take with the whole "home" thing. Should I go back to Canada? Should I stay here in the United States? I was conflicted. I didn't know what direction to take. I couldn't even go back to work. Thank goodness I had some savings to pay the rent and a supportive family that helped me financially. As you can imagine, I was messed up.

I no longer had goals or dreams because my husband and I did everything together. So when he was no longer with me—no longer alive, I was devastated. I thought, *What do I do now?* It felt like life took control of me by the neck, literally. So from then on, I had to muster up the energy to focus on not falling into a depression. That was my main objective. Whatever I must do, dance, go to the beach, go to the water, and eat ice cream, just don't fall into a depression!

In 2020, a lot of businesses were shutting down. They weren't hiring, and here I was, trying to figure out how I would be able to pay my rent. I couldn't find the energy to return to my stressful job. I felt like I was blocked from trying to find a different job—maybe I could find a job answering phone calls or just doing something routine. It seemed as if life just kept throwing curve balls at me.

Then, three months after my husband's passing, I came home from visiting his family. I was horrified to find my apartment had been damaged by a fire. It was dark and I didn't know how badly damaged my unit was. There was yellow tape blocking the entrance, but no one was around to tell me what was going on. I was freaked out and ended up calling a friend who helped me pack whatever clothes I could grab and welcomed me to stay at her place.

A few days later, thank God, the Red Cross was there to help me figure out where I could stay and what would happen next. They set me up in a hotel and I stayed there for two months. I spent many nights looking up at the ceiling, tears falling down my face because I couldn't believe this was my life. My husband and I had so many goals and so many dreams. Yet, now, I sit surrounded by most of my late husband's stuff, damaged by fire, smoke, and water.

Devastated, I knew I had to get out of this depression that was trying to drown me. So, I decided to bathe myself in sage. As I sat there in the warm water, thinking about everything that had transpired over the past few months, I cried out, "Please, get me through this. I want to get through this period. I cannot believe this is happening to me!"

After two months, I finally decided I could not continue living in a hotel room. All of this occurred during the height of COVID, as a result, a surge of employers needed contact tracers. So, I worked as a contact-tracer, enough to earn some income to get into an apartment. However, I lost my job the week I was supposed to relocate. But I moved into this beautiful apartment anyway. And that same day, I found a cat who became a part of my family. It helped me through some of the most challenging relapses and anxiety attacks I had ever been through.

Sometime later, I joined a program called Activating Your Vision, and at the end of that program, I had a collision with purpose. I discovered by helping families, starting with the matriarch of the family unit, I could help them build the courage to get through different trials of life. By helping these women believe they still look younger and more beautiful than ever and are able to live the life they desire, I realized that was my purpose.

Values and Beliefs

My deep compassion and love are values that drive me in pursuit of my purpose. I know how much love I can give to individuals such as my nieces, nephews, family, and significant other. I also tap into deep, unconditional love for myself. Authenticity also drives me in pursuit of my purpose. I find it challenging to work in spaces where I cannot be myself and be quirky. I can laugh over the silliest things. I love anything fun and joyful. But in spaces that are too serious, I fold totally. I strive to be a better person and help others live authentically. My deep-rooted values are the driving force for my purpose to come together and align.

Unique Contribution to Your Community

I hope to stop seeing family units at each other's throats, bickering, fighting, and arguing over the simplest things. I hope to see a turnaround where families can agree on simple things like what to eat for dinner, reach an agreement on where to go on vacation, or decide on how to spend time with each other. I want to see the family unit having fun, enjoying and understanding each other. Many family members need to understand that, as humans, we're constantly changing every day, minute, and hour. So it's important to ask questions, even if you think you know what the answer is going to be.

Too many families judge each other based on past experiences instead of reconnecting with the present.

Impact of My Purpose

I had a very challenging relationship with my biological mother; that was my story for years. I am probably psychologically still holding on to certain things. And based on the fact that I'm still going to therapy, I should continue to work through some additional stuff. I am now at a place in my life where I can look at my mother, and instead of thinking that she is treating me like a child, the child she left at two years old, I see her as wanting someone to vent to and blow off steam. My perception of who my mother is has shifted, and our relationship has improved significantly. We better understand each other, and when we don't, we ask each other questions. This shift in the relationship is amazing, because I feared she would pass away before we could improve our relationship.

Intentionality

For me, intentionality is following my values in life. It is one of the areas that I am working on improving in my life. There is a constant battle with wanting to please society instead of being true to who I say I am.

Live on Purpose

It is such a joy that you can see tangible results. It doesn't have to necessarily be someone coming to you to say thanks, but the results can come from self-realization like, *Wow! This person I worked with had their whole mood shifted. Oh, my gosh, they're smiling more!* Now I want to experience that over and over as I see how I can create sustainability within this purpose that drives me every day, every week, and every month to continue living it out.

How to Find Purpose

Do the work to bring yourself to stillness. I developed the practice of chanting, allowing for quieting the little chatter in my brain and getting centered. I am big on meditation, praying, and any little activity that will enable you to be still and remove the distractions, like the phone. You can develop a routine where you're praying, but many of us don't pray as we should. It's essential, especially in the morning. For example, as a little girl, I used to pray, "God, I promise never to lie again if only you give me ten dollars. I need these ten dollars to look nice at the school dance, and I promise I will never lie again." But that's like negotiating with a higher power, and that's different from how we should pray.

I believe that prayer should come from a place of surrender. "God, I want to thank you so much for allowing me this opportunity of greatness for me to look amazing at my dance and knowing that I'm going to be able to do a wonderful dance routine. I'm going to feel so amazing. And I want to give you thanks right now, right here, because I appreciate everything working out for me for the highest good. Amen." It's like an expectation in what is happening, and there's not much negotiation. If you're going to pray, make sure you are praying from your heart.

Purpose a Common Topic of Discussion

Purpose is not a common topic for discussion in my circle. The exception is my dad and second mom, whose own work is to help people tap into their higher purpose in their lifetime. They keep me connected to conversations around purpose in my circle.

I am dating now, and I ask guys, "Do you know your purpose?" Because to me, it's essential to know what my potential next life partner will be like. He has to know his purpose so I can either be a helping hand or a supporter. He might not know the answer, but if he doesn't consider exploring it a bit more, then it's usually a "no" for me.

How Do You Want to be remembered?

I want to be remembered as a very caring and encouraging individual. Someone who helped humanity to laugh more, to not take life so seriously, and to be vibrant. I want to be remembered as a soul sister who is right there whenever someone needs a hug or needs to feel appreciated.

Key Takeaway for the Reader

Those individuals who are unsure about their purpose should decide, right now, right here, what their purpose is. They can always build or change it. But as long as they have the basic general purpose in their brain, as they are living it out, it might evolve into something else. Just choose and get off the fence.

Aligning With God's Purpose

"God sits high, but He looks low," said my Mom.

Stacy Morse

Stacy Morse is an Educational Leadership Doctoral Student at Indiana Wesleyan University and the Founder and CEO of the Stacy Rena Morse (SRM) Foundation.

My Early Years

I am originally from Indianapolis, Indiana; I was raised with values by my parents and my family. My mom raised us with a lot of structure in the home and stressed education. I have siblings older than me; so there was a time when I was the only child at home with my parents during high school. During those years, it molded me to be able to do some self-reflection and grow into becoming my own person. This taught me much about what I wanted to do and who I wanted to be. This structure molded me for future success. Church was also important. I remember attending church every Sunday with my mom. That made me who I am today as well.

What Is Purpose

Your Purpose is what you are here for on this earth. What God placed you on this earth to do is solely your Purpose.

Knowing Purpose

It's important to know your Purpose on this earth. We are here to build up his kingdom, love each other and show that love through helping other people. I learned this at a young age in church. I believe that once you understand who you are and who you are from, you will understand that you are here to do a job, and that job is to fulfill whatever God has placed you here on this earth to do; that is your Purpose. You are not here forever; you're only here for a short while.

When you don't know your Purpose, you may not make the right decisions at first, like going to school. Why should I go to school? What should I major in for my bachelor's degree? When I first attended college, I didn't obtain my degree in what I initially went to school for. I recall saying, what do I want to do? I went to school for chemistry or pharmacy, or was it what my parents wanted me to do? I decided to pray for this because there was no fulfillment in attending these classes. I was not finding Purpose, which was not making me happy. I was thinking, *If I'm not happy, this is not what I'm supposed to be doing.* That's how I started learning to pray over what I am supposed to do to find my Purpose and not what everyone else is telling me what I am supposed to be doing.

My Purpose Defined

When I was a junior in college, I started praying over what I should do and what I was here for. So, my study started gearing toward the social work field. I specifically took one class at the University in Indianapolis, where I received my undergrad degree; I took a class with Dr. Mayer, who took us out into the communities. I had an epiphany when I took that class. I thought, *This is what I am supposed to be doing. I should be out in communities helping people.* That's when I realized what my Purpose was. I didn't precisely know the direction I was going in then. Still, I knew I would work in the lower marginalized types of communities, lower socio-economic communities. It was then I knew I would be in social work, and that is when I had my Collision with my Purpose.

Founder and CEO of Stacy Rena Morse Foundation

I am working on a doctorate in educational leadership. One of the program requirements is doing an actual research project. I wondered where I would want to do this research, and so I decided to do it in Twifo Hemang, Ghana, a community with fifty-two villages. When I initially decided to do the project, I contacted some community leaders. I initially spoke with Ma Vic, a member of the chief's team, and asked questions like: What are the issues you see in education? What are the problems that you are seeing in this community when it comes to education? How can I help? This led to many phone calls discussing the issues. Some concerns were that many kids needed transportation because they had to walk long distances to school, and didn't have shoes. Many students were required to wear school uniforms, but their parents are too indigent to pay for school fees or anything they needed for their learning materials.

Knowing this, I asked how I could help the community increase its enrollment. Ma Vic told me, "Many of the villages in Ghana have Non-Governmental Organizations (NGOs), but we don't have one. We need a little help with assisting the students with school uniforms and shoes." I decided to talk to some people to see how I could help; that's how this all transpired. I started an NGO, a non-profit organization that helps with the social wellbeing of others, and everyone wanted to come on board and support this cause. That's how it came to fruition.

If Not Ghana, Then Where?

In 2021, I went to Tanzania; we visited a few different Safaris. On the way home, we drove through some rocky roads where I saw kids sitting in the dirt, just playing and waving. I asked our driver where we were. He said, "We're in the villages," I'd never heard of the villages, but I asked if we could stop. He didn't think it was a good idea because we were still in the midst of the pandemic and needed to wear masks and be careful. I had my Covid shots, so I said it was okay. He stopped because I wanted to see some of the kids. Some of the children ran up to us and hugged us. They spoke Swahili and did not know English. The conditions there could have been better. After returning home, I could not get that Village out of my mind. I felt the need to do something there to help. Tanzania is where I initially should have done something, but my plans changed.

I contracted with a client in Ghana as a consultant for their palm oil company. When the gentleman hired me to work with his company, he did not say he was a member of the royal family. After the completion of the project, I told him I would be working on a research project and wanted to return to Tanzania to work on this project in the villages. He started laughing and said, let me reintroduce myself to you. He said, I'm from the royal family in Twifo Hemang. I still did not understand what that was about. So, he explained about the royal family, how they preside over the Kingdom Twifo Hemang, and that I can talk with his family members and King Otumfuo, the new chief. He further stated that they are implementing new changes in the community. That is how I got started. He connected me with Ma Vic, and I started communicating with her, and the next thing I knew I was on the phone with the King and everyone else from this community; it just took off from there.

Informed by an Event

A singular event informed my Purpose. The trip to Tanzania, Africa, in 2021 informed my Purpose. I went there during a difficult time in my life. I was going there to work. That specific drive going to the safari. We went to the Indian Ocean that day for a little while. I was looking at all the beauty, and I thought there was so much more to life that I should be doing; I was supposed to be happy. When I returned from Tanzania, I started praying a lot and asked God to show me what I should do. That trip inspired me to do what I am supposed to be doing, my Purpose. Upon returning, I made many personal decisions and choices to change the trajectory of my life and align with God's Purpose for me.

My Values and Beliefs

My mom passed away a year ago. She was a very good mom. I thank God for her. She was big on Love, always saying you must love people. She always told me, "Don't complain. You know someone's always doing worse than you. Thank God for everything you have." The values my mom instilled in me were to be there for people, help people, and care about people. She taught us to be good people. She never really wanted us to be materialistic or worldly. That's how I was raised, who I am, is the woman she wanted me to be.

Growing up, we were not always around our family and parents. Sometimes, you get a little off track when you get with people who may be different than you. But, I would always get back on track, knowing my mom would be saying, "This is not what I want you to do." That helped me. Just those values that she taught me growing up, that even though I may stray a little, I will always get back on the right path because I will remember that this is what she taught me and what she wanted me to do.

I always try to please her, ensuring she is happy. I grew up always saying God was watching me. My mom used to say, "God sits high, but he looks low." That stuck with me. I was always worried that I couldn't do this or that because I couldn't do things that were too bad. Those values made me who I am. It made me decide this is what I want to do. I learned from those values that my mom taught me about helping people. I enjoyed going into the communities. I enjoyed working with the families and some of the community centers. It just made me happy. And that stems from those values that my mom instilled in me.

How My Purpose Serves My Community

Many of the mothers in the community aren't literate. I would love to go back and work with some of the women in this community. I wanted to connect with the farmers so they could learn to grow their fruits and vegetables and start their little markets on the side of the roads. We can turn the community into a micro-community. After completing my dissertation and ensuring community sustainability, I aim to continue to evolve this community because it has so much potential. They have the resources there but need to learn how to utilize them.

I had lost my mom, but three weeks before that, I lost my niece to a tragedy in Indianapolis. She was twenty-seven years old. When I lost my niece, I kept asking, what should I do to honor my niece, De'ja Nicole? With that said, they need libraries in Twifo Humang. I asked Ma Vic, "Can we put little libraries throughout the community?" I get some books shipped from America, even though Twi is their local language, but many kids learn English as well.

"That's a great idea," she replied.

These libraries are now being implemented. The De'ja Nicole Library Nooks. Many kids will now have access to books; if they cannot get to a library, we will place them in schools and hopefully in churches. They will also have the ability to take books home with them.

I am working with some leaders here in Florida to see if they can help me ship barrels of books for the children. I also have had shoes donated. I need to organize everything in the United States to receive financial contributions. We can do more as far as helping with getting school uniforms made in the U.S. and then shipped over to the Village, along with some learning materials. I need simple things such as backpacks, pens, pencils, crayons, and paper. They are not asking for a lot, just the bare minimum. So, I would like to implement the drives for these donations. So far, we have succeeded in implementing some of the smaller projects we have been working on.

The Stacy Rena Morse (SRM) Foundation is organized as a Legal NGO Entity in Ghana. I have an SRM Foundation Ghana page on Facebook where we request books and supplies. Individuals have sent items to me here in the United States and directly to Ghana, where the team members work. We are not receiving any funding because I need to set up the organization to receive funding in the United States.

Currently, I am working on a shipping process for the barrels that is more cost-effective. We are still new, but some people contact us to ask where to ship items. Some individuals ship directly to Ghana through various means, except Amazon, which does not ship there.

Be Aligned with Purpose

Alignment with my Purpose allows me to wake up every day. That is when you are walking in your Purpose. It is me doing something that

I love, and it's impactful on the world. That makes me happy and has made me such a better person. I am proud of myself for the first time. So, aligning with what God has for me and being obedient to his call has made me happy and gratified. And I'm very fulfilled right now. Some days are only somewhat good. But I am still happy; I feel like I am still complete because I'm doing what God wants me to do. I am waking up not having some of the stress I used to have or being confused or in chaos. I can go to bed and say my prayers, and I am thankful and feel fulfilled at the end of the day.

Getting Back on Track

It takes a lot of prayer. The last year has been challenging for me because I lost my niece, mom, and oldest sister, all three weeks apart. I have been going through other things where I haven't been able to mourn them properly. Some days, I will wake up in this very dark place, but I pray. If I pray, I stay close to God, who has helped me. Instead of saying, "God, take all this away, I want everything to be okay." Teach me what I am supposed to learn from this. Just give me your strength, if I find myself in the same situation, I will know how to navigate through it. I am just trying to get to the other side. Once I get to the other side, everything will be okay.

A Discussion About Purpose

My sister, Dawn, and my best friend, Lori, from college are the only two people on this earth that I can honestly say that I have had conversations with regarding purpose. My sister is older than me, and

I have always looked up to her and tried to be like her. She is an excellent example for me. As we have gotten older, we now have conversations where the age gap seems to close again. Dawn is one of my support systems from whom I have gotten a lot of strength, especially since we have had a lot of family tragedies in the last year. Lori, my best friend, has stayed close to me throughout the previous year. I will call and tell her things, and she will say it was God.

My sister Sabrina is like the family's matriarch, well, for me anyway. Since my mom passed, she keeps me in alignment to ensure I stay on task with what I'm doing, or what I am supposed to be doing. Dawn is the one who's more intentional with having those conversations with me about Purpose.

Benefits of Discussing Purpose

Many people will benefit from discussions about Purpose because many people are frozen in time. I remember Dawn sending me a book about being unstuck, and it talks about Elijah and how he ran to the cave when he was running from Jezebel. After I read the book, I thought this book is so powerful. If everyone reads this book, they will realize they have a purpose in life and won't just be stuck somewhere.

So often, people don't know how to get to the other side to find their Purpose because they are trapped where they're at. They don't even know how to get to the point where they have a purpose in life, and to know their life would be so much better if they figured out what that Purpose is.

Knowing your Purpose is a mindset. I think once you realize there is more to life, and there is something you're supposed to be doing, and if you do that, it will make you happy. We all get up and go to work every day, but are you happy? But when you can get up every day, do whatever you are doing, and are eager for the next day to come because you're just happy, and you love what you are doing, then you have found your Purpose. That is when you finally see your Purpose.

Finding Purpose

Not everyone is into it; I'm not trying to teach everyone to be religious. You can read a lot of self-help books. But if you surround yourself with like-minded people and if you are the smartest, you are in the wrong room. Get around people with goals and aspirations and a sense of Purpose; you can learn from them. Surround yourself with people who can empower or improve who you are and get you on the right path. Those things will help you get on track, and then you will start to think, *Hey, what am I going to do? I'm helping this person, what should I do with my life?*

My Legacy

I want to be remembered as a woman of God, a great mother, and someone who impacted this world; someone who tried to build up God's kingdom and someone who is selfless and tried to make education the focal point for children. Knowledge is power, and if you're educating children and reflecting on letting them know that an education will help them to go far in life, that is my goal. That is something I want to be remembered for—as impacting children's lives and ensuring they know the importance of education to achieve personal goals and objectives. If I have done all of that, I will be happy.

Final Thoughts

It's all about believing in yourselves and being consistent in hard work and dedication so that you can do anything you want. Surround yourself with people who can make you better, positive people that want to help build you up because they are there. Place yourself in the right environment, surrounded by the right people, and learn as much as possible to elevate your life. Don't listen to the naysayers and negativity. You're going to go through some trials and tribulations in life. You'll go through some struggles, but you must have fortitude, tenacity, and faith to make it happen. There are going to be many days when it's hard, and you may not want to get out of bed. But you must talk to yourself daily and tell yourself, *I can do this and everything through Christ who strengthens me.* And it would be best if you moved forward. I believe in moving forward. I have been reading the Bible daily, and I always see it talks a lot about not looking back. So, no matter what you have done or the mistakes you may have made in the past, it doesn't matter where you are going, you can go to a higher height and move to better ground. So, you must believe in yourself, keep pushing forward and surround yourself with the right people.

I would love for everyone to go and research Twifo Hemang. I'm trying to be as impactful as I can in this community. The children need so much in this community. I want them to get a good education. I want them to have good schools without sitting on the ground in the mud on rainy days and have restroom facilities. So, my most significant focus right now is on the children in the Village. It is not about me. I always tell my staff, "Let's make the right decisions regarding the children." I want to increase education outcomes in this community, that is my Purpose.

If Not Me, Then Who

"If not me, then who? I don't ever want to be a victim of "bystander syndrome."

Imari Harris

Imari Harris is a student at the University of Florida majoring in political science. Imari plans to continue her education by attending law school to earn her Juris Doctor degree. Currently, she's a litigation clerk working for a local law firm. She has a passion for inspiring young women to pursue careers in the criminal justice field through her Community Service Initiative, #LegislateHER, a mentorship program she created for young girls to explore careers in the criminal justice field.

My Early Years

I grew up dancing. My mom put me in the studio when I was two years old. So, being on stage feels like my home, and I love expressing myself to people that way. Though, if you ask my mom, she will tell you that I've always wanted to be a lawyer since I was five years old and knew what college was. I told her that I was going to Harvard

Law School and would be a big-shot New York attorney. Unfortunately, my dreams of being a New York attorney were squashed when I visited New York. The city is too fast for me; I don't think I could live out there.

I've always had a passion for law and government. I believe that voices are best heard when they have a seat at the table. And if not me, then who? I don't ever want to be a victim of "bystander syndrome." I don't want to think someone else is going to solve this problem or that someone else is going to come along and be a better fit.

Also, I never want to fall prey to the mindset of "I can't because I'm not ready." Ask yourself, "What can I do to get ready?" You're never really going to be ready. You miss out on so many moments, opportunities, and doors that can be opened for you waiting for the right time. The right time may never come for you to start something. You just have to keep fighting until you see the results that you want. If you truly believe in something, you can't let up off the gas pedal until your goals are accomplished.

Competition Time

Currently, I am the local title holder for the Miss City Beautiful 2023. I relinquished the Miss Florida Gator 2023 title. It's now the season for the local competition for the Miss Florida Scholarship, which is through the Miss America organization. If I were to be crowned the new Miss Florida, I would compete at the Miss America pageant. Our organization does not compete internationally. So, the highest I can achieve is Miss America. It's so amazing seeing so many bright and intellectual young women all in the same room. They all have different platforms and different social movements they support.

There is a talent section where I write and perform monologues, then change my clothes, get back on stage, and talk for thirty seconds about "Vote Pink," which is a mentorship program that I created for young girls to explore different fields in the criminal justice region. This is the only space where I can be theatrical and show off my legal side. Through pageantry, I've been able to keep up my theatrics. I keep writing monologues, and now I have a shiny crown and a brand-new platform to speak on.

I hope to inspire young women the way I was inspired when I was younger, because I didn't have someone who looked like me doing the same things I was looking forward to. Through pageantry, #LegislateHER, and literally everything I do, I want to be the representation my younger self did not have. I have two beautiful nieces and a beautiful baby sister. They see people in our family and women who look like them pursuing politics, law, government, and pageantry because we are rare in these fields. It's sad because it's not for lack of trying or lack of belief, it's just a lack of representation. If more girls were to start competing or attending law school and exploring careers in politics, law, and government, we would see our young generation coming up behind us. Sometimes you must see someone do it to believe you can do it yourself. If not me, then who? That's just the mindset I've had for a long time.

Purpose Defined

Purpose is passion plus action. Your passion is what you love doing. I love everything related to law and government. I have found my Purpose by actively creating mentorship programs, joining clubs and organizations on my campus, being involved in my internship as a litigation clerk, and then continuing to spread that message through my role as a title holder in the Miss America Organization. When you are genuinely passionate about something, you must put action behind it for it to be your Purpose as you are actively working towards improving yourself.

Passion, Practice, and Purpose

Passion inspires you, something you believe you're good at. My passion is law and government, and then theater, I put that into practice through pageantry. I get to talk about #LegislateHER, in which I lecture on the Big Three—Courts, Law Enforcement, and Politics.

Importance of Purpose

Purpose is important, but I also want people to know that sometimes your calling changes, and it's okay to feel like you don't understand why you are here. I don't think people should be caught up trying to determine why they exist but should pursue their passions however they see fit. Some people may think, *Oh, this is my purpose, so I only have to do this one thing for the rest of my entire life.* But that's not true because your calling is what you love to do. I love theater, so I am passionate about it, so I write and perform monologues when I compete for local or state titles and, hopefully, a national title one day. You can have multiple goals and passions at the same time. Once we realize a large community is passionate about the same things, more people will start to put actions behind their passions. That will give it relevance and make a significant impact, and it's fulfilling the reason I was created.

I believe it's also possible to have overarching purposes which may require different ways to get there. Initially, pursuing law just started with being a political science major as an undergrad. Then, I ended up with an internship as a litigation clerk. Now, I'm actively studying for the Law School Admissions Test (LSAT), and I am getting ready to put myself into law school. Being able to speak about law and government through pageantry and interacting with different organizations on campus, these are all different ways that I'm pursuing the same goal of spreading my message that criminal justice is important and that more women should be involved.

My Inspiration

My mom inspired me to pursue a higher education. She has a master's degree in nursing. However, I didn't have anyone in my circle of family and friends who wanted to pursue law and government as I did. The first time I saw somebody I was genuinely inspired by in the political realm was former first lady Michelle Obama. She is amazing. She took on her role like she was an elected official. She had her agenda and different programs she was overseeing because she was passionate about them. Now, of course, we have Vice President Kamala Harris.

I love being able to see the black community thrive. It is so important because we don't want to fall prey to the stereotypes hanging over our heads. The more we show that we are more than the stereotypes, and bigger than the problems people put on our backs, and show our younger generations these are not things that you must listen to, we can do amazing things and ignore all the haters telling us that we can't.

What Informs My Purpose?

When I was in the seventh grade, my aunt was murdered. She was out with family and friends. Two men started arguing, guns were drawn, and she became a casualty. That was the first time I had dealt with the grief of losing somebody close to my heart. The prosecuting attorney who worked with my family was kind and empathetic. It was so nice and refreshing to see somebody cared that much about our situation when they did not have to.

At twelve years old, I knew everything that happened in her case because I was a very good eavesdropper. I was not allowed in the courtroom, after all, I was too young. My mom didn't want me or my brother there, but I listened to her when she talked on the phone to the attorney. My papa and my grandma understood everything because the attorney explained it to them very well; and I, also, understood him.

I believed I would be the one to put the man away who killed my aunt. I thought, *I'm going to law school, and I'm going to get my degree. I will be in the courtroom, and he will go to jail, and I will be the one to put him there.* However, I am still an undergrad. I have yet to make it to law school. But he has been in prison a long time.

The Values and Beliefs that Drive My Pursuit of Purpose

I have two nieces, Kaidence, and the youngest is Kinsley. I know they look up to me. I didn't believe it when I was younger because I was still in elementary school when my niece and younger sister were born. My older sister, my nieces' mom, and my dad always told me that I had to watch what I said and did because they looked up to me. I would always say, "They don't look up to me. I'm just here. They don't care about what I'm doing." But as I got older, I realized what they told me was true.

My sister sent me videos of my niece watching me at the Miss Orlando pageant. She was so engaged with what I was doing, she loved absolutely everything. So, when I finally got my crown, she was thrilled. She said, "Oh my, God, my TT is a princess." Seeing her being overjoyed at watching what I am doing warms my heart. I love seeing that light in her eyes.

I got a chance to meet a little girl named Cadence at the Miss Orlando Pageant, who is no relation to me or my Kaidence. I was the first runner-up at the pageant, but I did not win a title. However, she ran up and asked, "Can I take a picture with you?" I started sobbing.

I told her, "Listen, y'all are why I continue to do what I do." Seeing little kids and their faces light up when they realize, *Oh my God, she's doing that. I can do that, too.* That little girl made me sob. Through tears, I said, "Oh, my gosh, thank you so much. You're making me feel like a celebrity."

She replied, "Well, you are."

My mom interjected, "Stop crying. I'm trying to take your picture."

After that, I competed at every local event that I could before I finally won. I received the David Davis Scholarship at the best Gainesville competition—second runner-up at Miss Sport Citrus, and Fourth Runner Up at the Miss University of Florida. I did not place at all at Miss South Florida. I was the first runner-up at Miss Orlando. Then, when we did Sweeps, our digital competition, I won the title of Miss Florida Gator. I was determined and just kept going until there were no other events left for me to compete in within the state of Florida.

I made a vision board for the first time. I wrote down all my goals and Bible verses that are fueling my determination to reach those goals. I wrote my vision on my board December 31st of last year. I will win the title of the Miss America organization.

I am a family-orientated person, I call my mom and dad every day to tell them about what's happening in my life. They are more excited about my competitions than I am; they even made me T-shirts for graduation. They are my biggest fans; I have no idea where I would be without them. I love my relationship with the rest of my family, too, even though I may not speak to them often. They're amazing people who are so loving, giving, and so supportive of the things I do. When I compete, I am only on stage for thirty seconds, yet I have family that travel from various states just to be there for me. I am thankful I have that support system. I honestly have no idea where I would be without it.

Utility of Education

Education is power, especially in America. The more knowledge you attain, the more power you have. The most powerful piece of knowledge or information that you can have is to be informed about politics, to be informed about your rights, and to be informed about the laws that affect you and your everyday life. I think that by creating a mentorship program like #LegislateHER and by working with people like the Women's Student Organization and Black Student Union and all the different organizations on our campus, it is important to show students that may not have known that they can still pursue law or politics with the major they are already in. Law school has yet to have specific prerequisites to be enrolled. It's not like med school, where you have to be a pre-med major. I could have literally majored in dance and still gone to law school if I wanted to or majored in the arts and still went to law school.

I know it's a fear of many young people who may not have had the experience as I did to speak in front of crowds. Being in the Academy of Law and Government in high school, our academy director did not do well with shy kids. She would say, "You are in this academy; you are going to learn how to speak in front of a crowd. You might not like it, but you're going to do it. If someone calls on you to speak, you won't be afraid of it anymore." If you can express yourself properly, you will not be misunderstood or misrepresented, which can happen if you are not able to communicate effectively. The way people perceive you is the way doors and opportunities open for you.

My Interest in Law and Government

I've always been interested in law and government; I don't need a degree or a law degree to be a politician. However, there's a lot of misinformation on the Internet, so I would rather go to school and learn it from someone who knows what they're talking about, which will help me to understand the system better. It will give me different avenues to go into politics. With a Juris Doctorate degree (J. D.), you don't have to be an attorney. You can do many things with a J. D. without passing the bar or becoming a practicing attorney. That's the avenue that I want to go down because what better career than to get paid to speak than a lawyer or a politician?

I went to a hearing in Tallahassee, Florida, in the House of Representatives where they were talking about House Bill (H. B.) 99. There were over 200 people that showed up and spoke about how this bill would impact them and how it would affect their jobs, their education, their programs. My mentor and I went and spoke out against the bill. It was so amazing to see not only students but professors present.

There is power in your voice! Otherwise, nobody is going to know what you are thinking. Nobody will know your passions if you do not open your mouth and say something. Even if you do not have voting power, you can pick up a phone and call your legislator. You can send emails, canvass people, and inform people with your knowledge, because connecting with people, is the most powerful thing we can do as citizens.

The Impact of Living on Purpose

I am filling out paperwork to work with Pace, a school for young girls that are often seen as troubled. I must get vetted through the juvenile justice system, get fingerprinted, and do everything requested of me. I have been working with the program director there, and she's excited to see #LegislateHER finally come to their school. There is a women's excellence program in Seminole County, and seeing the excitement around my program excites me.

On Saturdays, I go to the YMCA, where I talk to many little kids. I tell them all the great things about the criminal justice system and ask them what they want to do when they grow up. People don't know how vast this field is. For example, if you're passionate about medicine and want to do something in criminal justice, there are avenues for you to do that. If you want to be a nurse, you can still be in the criminal justice system. You can be a nurse in a corrections facility or in a juvenile facility. You can still make those connections and impact this field, while pursuing your passion. I think people don't go into criminal justice because they don't know about these options. But by talking to different communities, especially kids, it helps to fuel their passion.

As I mentioned earlier, I knew I wanted to be a lawyer when I was five, but not everybody knows at a young age what they want to be. I know it's so cliche, but I watched Law and Order Special Victims Unit every time it came on, and there was an attorney, Rafael Barba, on the show. And the actor that plays him is Raul Esparza. I know it was fake, but seeing the passion behind his actions, I knew that real people do that daily. Seeing that on television and then meeting and talking with real attorneys who do that every day is amazing.

The Big Three

If you are interested in a career in criminal justice, there are three areas you might consider. The first one is the courts. You can be a stenographer or a court reporter, a bailiff, which is a police officer that works within the courts, a judge, a lawyer, or law enforcement. Secondly, you can work as a military policeman, a patrol officer, or in the sheriff's department. And third, you can get involved in politics— local politics, state politics, and national politics. There are so many avenues you can go down in criminal justice; however, these are the main three that people see the most.

A Discussion About Purpose

Purpose is a common discussion among my peers because we're all in school and still trying to figure out what we're super passionate about. Most of my friends are Science, Technology, Engineering, and Mathematics (STEM) majors. I have a lot of mechanical engineering and engineering friends. As for me, I am a liberal arts science student. I love writing essays. I love researching and presenting things verbally rather than computing numbers and code. I saw one of my friend's homework, and he was coding something, and I said, "That is not English. That is not normal math. I have no idea what you are doing." But my friends feel the same when I tell them how I write legal briefs or prepare for mock court tournaments. It's interesting to see how different we are but still very similar because we're all friends. It's cool that we can connect on one level and pursue our Purpose differently.

Living With Purpose

What I mean by living with purpose is being disciplined within undisciplined things. It aligns my day-to-day activities with how I want my overall life. It's not a disciplined activity to sit down and watch Netflix. However, if you have a schedule for yourself where you say, from this time to that time I'm going to do these specific things, and you do it, that's being disciplined in your day-to-day activities, which is so important.

I am bad at keeping up with my regular schedule. I feel like when I have a break, I take one forever. Everything still gets done, but I could be more disciplined when doing things that don't necessarily have a specific purpose but fuel my social battery and engage with more like-minded people.

Discover Purpose

My most significant advice is to spend one-on-one time with people you see doing what you're interested in. Reach out to the communities on your campus, city, and state. When you see somebody doing what you want to do, it is not necessary for you to convert yourself into that person, because it is very important for you to remain strong in your identity. But when you see students on campus organizing how you want to organize or being a part of organizations like Phi Alpha Delta, a pre-law organization on our campus, reach out to them and say, "Hey, this is something I'm interested in. How did you get involved in this?" Even if you don't necessarily want to join the same organization, it sets you up for success so that you now know how to communicate with different people with the same mindset as you.

My Legacy

I want to be remembered as a community leader. I aim to be engaged with communities outside of my own. I have found myself in Club Creole; my good friend is the organization's president, and she is teaching me how to speak Creole and about Haitian culture. I have just learned so much just by being there, just by helping them with the things I can. For example, since they know that I'm very passionate about pageantry, I helped them organize their pageant.

I want people to remember the advice that I gave them—to keep being themselves. No matter how many doors are closed in front of you, if you turn around, one opens behind you. There may be one that opened to the side of you. If you keep looking at the door that is closed, you'll miss the opportunities being granted to you. "No" does not mean impossible. It just means "No, not right now." It doesn't mean you can't do it eventually. Had I stopped the first time someone told me no, I would have never accomplished the achievements that I have.

You will be told "no" many times before you finally get told "yes." If you accept "no, as not right now," instead of "no, you can never do it," you'll see so many opportunities granted to you. Who knows, maybe that "no" was protecting you from something. Perhaps you didn't need to join that club, or you didn't need to work for that company. Now, you have better opportunities that you would have never seen if you continued to think, *No, never,* instead of, *No, not right now.*

The biggest takeaway is literally that "No" does not mean impossible. It does not mean give up, it simply means *"No, not right now."*

My Parting Words

I want to encourage people to continue being themselves. I know that, specifically within my age group, we're all college-age kids. We are either preparing for grad school, preparing to come into college, preparing to leave college, or going into the real adult world where we have to do everything ourselves. As somebody who has struggled with their mental health in the past, when you cling to the people who truly love you, and are truly supportive, even in your downfalls, even in your moment of crisis, that is how you overcome that mental hurdle. That is how you come out from under the weight that is bearing down on you. That is how you come out of the darkness. When you lean on those people who are allowing you to rely on them, you throw your entire body weight on them for as long as you must. Find people who will allow you to vent, it is a great form of therapy and a way to talk about all of the things that are stressing you out; and you'll feel better afterward. Just remember to take time for yourself and focus on your mental health. Then, when they need support from you, be there for them.

Lastly, it was great to use my title as Miss Florida Gators for something good. Speaking about "Purpose" is one of the first things I did in this role. I cannot wait to share this topic with everybody who is super excited to see me do things with #LegislateHER. I encourage everyone to find a friend that is super passionate about the things you're passionate about and pursue your Purpose. At the end of the day, there's never going to be a "right" time, but if you start right now, something will come to fruition.

SECTION II

Purpose By Design

Purpose by Design is a path where individuals chart their course in life, sculpting their aspirations and ambitions with precision and intentionality. Individuals deliberately and strategically craft their life's journey to align with a greater sense of meaning and significance.

Purpose by Design involves deeply understanding one's values, passions, and talents and aligning them to create meaning. It requires foresight, self-reflection, and unwavering commitment to stay true to one's vision.

Purpose by Design is a journey of fulfillment and authenticity, where each step is taken with intention, and every action is a brushstroke on the canvas of their unique life story. Individuals who experience a Collision With Purpose through Purpose by Design are empowered to navigate challenges with resilience in the face of adversity, which fuels focused determination.

Dr. Laxley W. Stephenson

How To Stay Alive

"Purpose for some people is figuring out how to stay alive today, and the day after, and the day after that. It is the reality of many people."

Pavlina Bozhkova

Pavlina Bozhkova is from Bulgaria, a small country located on the Balkan Peninsula in Europe near Ukraine. She is a film director, screen director, and advocate for social change. She is an educator and also enjoys teaching Spanish and Bulgarian languages.

My Early Years

Even though I lived behind the Iron Curtain, my childhood was peaceful and happy. Bulgaria was a socialist country with great censorship, restrictions, and strong Soviet propaganda. All this hindered the normal development of the country and the people, but I did not know this because I was a child living in a family with a lot of love and support, and we were happy.

My Purpose

My purpose has always been to have the opportunity to have a job that I love. Perhaps, now I am much more aware of this purpose, but I unconsciously adhered to it in the past. What I like doing is be involved in the arts—theater, and cinema. Even when I was in school, I wrote scripts and stage plays. Later, I went to study cinematography at a university, and now this is my job—I'm a film director and screenwriter. I love doing documentaries—observing and telling stories about the every-day people, their lives and relationships with others. When we see their lives, we see the lives of society as a whole. This is what I love to do with all my heart. And I fight to be able to do it. That is my purpose.

Why do I Have to Fight for this Purpose?

The limitations for me are not a few. I am a woman, and women in Bulgaria not only have to raise and educate their children, but also take care of the home. At the same time, they must find strength and motivation to develop in their profession. The film director's profession is difficult. It requires a lot of concentration, dedication, investment of time, and, at many moments, detachment from the family and its problems. So, it's a real struggle. And I haven't stopped fighting for my purpose—to do what I love, to be a film director.

It was easy for me to determine my purpose because I was interested in this field from a young age, and it was not so difficult to decide that this is what I want to connect my life and efforts with. I realize that is not the case with everyone. The truth is that our lives are a series of small goals. We rarely sit down to think if we have any great global purpose. We often set short-term goals that we follow in one way or another, preventing us from having that big global purpose. But for everyone, no matter how big their goal is, having one is important. It is important to decide where our heart leads, what we are good at, what we can do to help others, and follow our plan.

Family and Purpose

I am a mother, and it has always been important to me that my children have a purpose. I have a son who is nineteen, another son who is seventeen, and a daughter who is nine. Small, big, it doesn't matter. The important thing is that they have something to strive for. I have tried to educate them that anything is achievable; you must know how to do it. If you know what you want to achieve, you can take the next step to make a plan. When we have a plan that could be changed in the process of completing the goal, it gives us support, helps us distribute our efforts, and allows us at different times to see if we are making good progress or whether something is stopping us. First, we need to find what would make us truly happy, and second, make a plan. And then, the specific steps of the plan follow.

Education and Purpose

I have to put education first. It is the first step a person must take, no matter what profession it is. Education provides the base and initial knowledge to develop in the future. Since my purpose is related to professional realization, the places I receive information, motivation, and inspiration to continue developing are related to this profession. It is very important to me, and I want my children to get an education that would be useful to them. I encourage them to find what they like so that I can support them in getting the knowledge they need. After getting an education, one continues to search. Many institutions, organizations, and events are related to my profession from which I get inspiration, more knowledge, and opportunities to share my interests with others. They are a steady support in pursuing my goal of being a female director.

First, a person should believe in him or herself. We must think that we can handle it, have the strength and support, and deserve to handle it, develop it, and stand up for our dreams and plans. Believing in yourself is important, but it's also a very difficult thing. In the beginning, one tends to doubt oneself, one's powers, one's abilities, but what can save you is taking the first step. After that, take the second step, and then, the third. Experience alone will convince you that you can. He who believes in himself can take the first steps, albeit with uncertainty, but it is very important. It's easier from there. I'm sure. There is always someone to help you. Circumstances had occurred in my life so that even when something seemed impossible to me to achieve a certain goal, at some point, without my expectation, someone appeared who was just there to help me. Maybe it is the finger of fate, or it's just part of the global plan for me, for us.

Family and Purpose

I am a mother, and it has always been important to me that my children have a purpose, their own goals and direction in life. I have a son who is nineteen, another son who is seventeen, and a daughter who is nine. I think when it comes to teenagers, it is very important they learn to achieve small goals, but small or big, it doesn't matter. The important thing is that they have something to strive for, to believe in themselves, to believe in the process, to believe that it is possible, but also to see that not everything is achieved easily.

I have tried to educate my children that anything is achievable; you must know how to do it. First, we need to find what would make us truly happy. If you know what you want to achieve, then the specific steps to accomplish your objective should follow. Even when we have a plan, it can be changed in the process of completing the goal. A plan gives us support, helps us distribute our efforts, and allows us at different times to see if we are making good progress or whether something is stopping us.

There are always difficulties, but not stopping in the face of those trials is a small victory and is very important for you as a person. Because if today, you manage something small and it gives you confidence, then, one day, when the obstacle in front of you is big, you will still carry that confidence that you can handle it. All this is learned first within the family.

Purposed to Help Others

I feel I have many purposes. When I see a problem, it's important to me to act on it, to try and solve it. For example, because of the war in Ukraine, there are a lot of refugees who are in need. I thought one way to help is to teach them the Bulgarian language which will help them to integrate easier and find work, make friends, live in Bulgaria, and move about safely. So, along with ten volunteer teachers, we started offering Bulgarian language courses online. This platform can be used for any ethnic group or other minority groups. The Ukrainian situation is urgent and requires urgent actions.

The Benefits of Knowing My Purpose

I'm practical. I can plan my steps, choose my actions, and find collaborators to help me. Knowing my purpose allows me to make goals, then act on them. I'm very happy with the people around me. So, I choose those friends to collaborate with to help me. I specifically look for people who share my ideas and whose purpose is very close to mine.

What do you Want People to Take Away?

Life is easier when a person has a purpose and a plan. It sounds a bit pretentious, but it's the very truth. When a person has faith in his plan, life has structure. Life has meaning and development. This is also the feeling that we are part of the world, that we are part of the process of life. We are not excluded! We are not just observers somewhere on the sidelines, but we are active participants in life and the development of the world. Having a purpose is as vital as breathing, eating, and moving. Purpose gives life because it gives meaning. So, keep moving. Keep doing something and everything will be alright.

God Chose Me

"God is no respecter of person, and
I felt humbled that he chose me to do this work."

Yves Foster

Yves Foster is a Wife, Mother, Minister, License Professional Counselor, and The Founder and Executive Director of Abundant Well Foundation, A Nonprofit Charity located in Marietta, Georgia.

My Early Years

I am one of two. I only have one sister. My mom only had the two of us. And to hear her tell the story, she was never able to carry her pregnancies to term. Every time she became pregnant, she lost the baby; so when she speaks, she says, you are the only two that the Lord spared and gave me. I was the firstborn. My little sister came a year later. We grew up with a normal family dynamic—Mom and Dad. My dad was a disciplinarian. He did not spare the rod—and neither did my mom. But she was more subtle with her discipline the first few years of my life. We went to Catholic school. Then, when we moved to New Jersey, I started going to a public high school. After high school,

I went to Florida for college, met my husband, and got married. We've been married for the past thirty years, and in January, we celebrated our thirtieth anniversary.

Looking at the Broad Definition of Purpose

One would not often think about their Collision with their Purpose, at least not in their everyday life. Sitting and thinking about defining Purpose, I referred to the dictionary where it is defined as the reason something is done or created or the reason for its existence elsewhere.

When the term Purpose comes to mind, I think intentionality, determination, and direction. I see what I am called to do, like a propeller, it is something that drives me forward, something that can answer the reasons for my actions, giving my life meaning, and helping life make sense. The why of what I do may determine the journey and the road that I may take so that I can fulfill my calling. That is how I define Purpose.

Understanding My Purpose and Others Understanding Theirs

Intentionality is an important element in defining one's Purpose; it helps to give life meaning. It makes life make sense. In my field as a professional counselor, I do encounter quite a few individuals who do not think they have a God given reason for being alive. The only solution they seem to think about is suicide or some form of self-harming because they don't believe they have a reason to be around. It reinforces my thinking that it is so important to be intentional about knowing the reason you were created. Thinking about this topic is so crucial for us to understand that we, first, do have a reason for our existence, and second, understand what that is, or at least have enough curiosity to seek and to engage with ourselves so we can get to that place where we have clarity as to why we are here.

I don't believe purpose is a destination. It is part of our journey, so we can get to that place where we are at peace with ourselves, where we are one with ourselves, and we can function in this life the way we were meant to. That is another aspect of my definition of finding my destiny and understanding the importance and value of knowing the true essence of my life. You may try to do many things, you may be very determined, be a go-getter, and a hard worker. However, because you're not working for the reason you were created, you end up feeling like you have failed.

Defining My Purpose

My family and I came from Florida, so, everyone I knew, the platform I had, my network,

everything was left back there. When we first moved to Georgia, I was thinking, *I'm new here. I don't know anyone; I don't have a network or a platform; I don't even have a community that I can call my own, that I could lean on and lean into. How on Earth am I going to do this?* I set everything aside and went on doing something else. I started quite a few things that failed because I didn't necessarily want to embrace my calling.

However, being informed about events and understanding my destiny fueled my sense of Purpose. I started going on a yearly mission trip with a missionary group. In 2016, we went to a region in Haiti known as "Gardere." It is in a remote location, high in the mountains, and it's hard to get to because it sits at the top of the mountain. There are no paved roads, so at certain points we had to get out of the vehicle to lighten the load so the bus could continue. The first time I went to Gardere, it blew my mind because it showed me that God is no respecter of person, and I felt humbled that he chose me to do this work at this time. I am a counselor; I'm a professional. Now I am leading this nonprofit organization, and it never dawned on me that this would be the direction destiny would take me. However, that is where I find the most satisfaction.

The Pursuit of My Purpose Has Impacted Others in My Community

As a professional, there is a purpose connected to my actions. I want to help the company I work for succeed in what they do. So, now their needs become my Purpose. To be the best employee, I ensure that the clientele I see daily gets what they need from me. As a mother, my primary objective is to make sure that I raise children to become productive citizens in society, strong individuals of value who value themselves. In my role as a wife, I want to be the best partner to my husband.

The Values and Beliefs That Drive My Pursuit of Purpose

What informs the reason for my existence is obedience to the Father. During the yearly missionary trips to Gardere, I felt humbled that the Creator saw fit to draw me into this work, these people are not my family. However, I felt a connection to the place, to the people, and to the children. So, we went there and ministered to them. The ministry conducted a health fair, distributed food and clothing, provided medications because quite a few of the children seemed to have a lot of skin related issues. There was no sound structure where they could come and worship, and where they worshiped also served as the school for the children. The ministry went ahead and built a school, When school started, it seemed like a lifeline for the community, however they weren't consistently coming to school. We found out later that the parents were afraid the children may faint on the way due to hunger, so they kept them home, and that is where that drive started.

I wanted to build a canteen for them, for the school, so that those children could come in and have a hot meal. In our case, it means two hot meals, breakfast, and lunch, then sending them home. The area does not have water either, which is another part of our project. Once I'm done building the canteen and working on the operation of that canteen, outfitting it, and then doing the monthly feeding, the next project will be to bring water to that region. I will say once I started doing that, the connection that I felt to it, the drive that I have, the passion that I have for the children, for the region, for the possibility of what can be is what drives me, and it will continue to guide me until I see it to fruition.

Walking in Purpose

It's one thing to talk about some things, but it's a whole different thing when you get your hands in there and watch it take shape. That is where I'm at and where my Purpose came from. It came from one of my mission trips and meeting those people with their dire needs, and thinking if you don't do something, an entire generation may perish, but you can do something.

Here I am, living, walking, and aligning myself with my Purpose, which brings less frustration to my life. Sometimes, what we are called to do doesn't come how we expect it to; having a nonprofit organization is not what I thought about when planning my life. I did not expect Purpose to come out in that package, but that's how it came. When you come to your calling and finally figure it out, you don't want to get to that place all battered and angry because you wasted so much time doing everything except what you were supposed to do. Again, thinking about living my life purposefully helps me feel less frustrated. You see, I can rest knowing that I am doing precisely what I am supposed to be doing. I no longer must latch onto someone else's Purpose.

We often cling to somebody else's dream because we fail to realize our own. Sometimes, we fail to allow ourselves to walk into what we are supposed to walk into. Something may happen, and you may think nothing of it. However, it was a form of preparation for where you would be a week from now, a month from now, or a year from now. It could be a class you needed to take, a workshop you attended, or a mission trip. Somebody may say, "Why don't you come with me and see what we're doing over here?" You may not realize this is part of your preparation for where you should go. You're doing everything you need to do, not fighting against the waves but going with it. And that, to me, is walking in your Purpose and doing everything, whatever you need to do at that moment, so you can get to the next step, whatever is going to take you to the next level, whatever is going to take you closer to realizing the reason for your existence. That is walking in your Purpose.

We had our board meeting, and I was sharing some of what I did, and then it dawned on me, oh, wow. Everything that I have done so far is to ensure that Abundant Well Foundation succeeds, to ensure that we do not get in trouble with the state of Georgia, so we don't get in trouble with the IRS, so we don't get in trouble with the laws of the state, whether it's soliciting, finding other nonprofits to partner with, establishing a Web presence, etc. My aim right now is to make sure that it will succeed. Why? Because a group of children are waiting and counting on it, even though they don't have access to it. However, whatever is going to come out of that is going to benefit them.

Everything that I do right now, regardless of how big or small it is, is to make sure that our foundation succeeds so that I can meet those needs. So, sometimes, what we call missteps are our preparation for the work ahead. Right? To get us to that one thing—that is our Purpose. And in saying that, the organization must succeed not because I want it to but because of the needs, service, and work the organization is called to do. That is so important.

Sometimes we busy ourselves so much that we don't understand or cannot articulate why you exist here on earth. I am a great proponent of mindfulness. The things that we should be capturing, we don't capture because we are so busy; we rip and run, and never sit still. I believe in stillness. You see, I have a son. I tell him all the time, Honey, be still with yourself because whatever you need will come to you; to receive whatever is yours, to have a purpose, direction, and guidance, you must be still. You must sit still to find what it is and know the next step you must take.

It is so hard to focus. And it's hard to think when there are so many voices coming at you all at once and from all over the place, our world is noisy. Many things stimulate us, and none of those things get us where we need to be, or places us in the state of mind we need to be in to discover. Because here is the thing, you don't realize your value outside of yourself, but within. It's not what everybody else is saying, you are so great at this, or that, and the other, but we must be able to sit still with ourselves to find which direction we need to go. It won't come from outside, some people might not want to hear that, but for some, it might be just what they need to hear. You need to be still with yourself and at least start allowing your voice to come out, so you can listen, and see, and understand and determine which direction you need to go and find your way through.

Purpose Is a Common Discussion with Family and Friends

There aren't enough conversations around Purpose within the context of families or school. It is important that we start the conversation at home when the child is still learning about his/her world because the future generation will lead and run things. In the family setting, we must talk about our reason for our existence because young people need guidance, and they need to be allowed to explore until they discover their true calling, and that is where parents can provide that space within the family context.

Let's talk about it. What's happening? Why am I here? What are you thinking about? Where do you plan on being? We need not impose what we believe on others, which brings me back to when I mentioned my son. I am always telling him, Honey, follow your voice; follow your dream. But to find your voice, you must learn to be still and silent. Spend some time with you, turn the TV off, turn off your phone, and be still within yourself; you will find directions. You will discover which direction to go, but you must be still long enough to listen.

You must be intentional about living your Purpose. You must be deliberate about the steps you take, especially once you find something that you're passionate about, that rises in you. You do want to be deliberate about the actions you start taking so you can move toward that purpose. Again, you may have an idea, however, if you're not willful about this, then you will probably find yourself going around a never-ending circle, wasting time with frustration, doing many things that have nothing to do with what you're supposed to be doing.

Time is of the essence in our world nowadays, and how we manage that time is vital. Purpose is not a destination, right? It is part of an overarching design that moves us forward. First and foremost, be still within yourself to find your calling. Shutting out the noise can be challenging, but you owe it to yourself. You owe it to your future self to shut out today's noise so you can get to where you can find what you're supposed to do.

My Parting Words I Leave on Purpose

I will leave you with this: enjoy the journey; however, it can get bumpy, but do what it takes to bring you that much closer to where you need to be. The thing is, I'm discovering new things every day about who I am, and I am learning new things about myself, which is another upside to finally embracing my purpose. I'm becoming more resourceful than I thought; perhaps I have more support than I think, and I can be trusted to do this. Again, along the way, you are making wonderful discoveries about yourself and learning about who you are and who you are becoming, so my parting word is that it is important to bring others into this conversation. It's a conversation that should be continuous because helping young people find their destiny is fundamental for them and humanity. Again, what's locked up inside of them may benefit somebody else, and if they don't have a safe place to explore and give them a chance to discover and manifest it, then we are the poorer for it.

Walking in My Purpose

"Look, I'm doing this because I love you!"

Mr. Augusta Foster III

Mr. Augusta Foster III is a father, a program analyst at Delta Airlines, a mental health advocate, and a social change advocate.

My Early Years

I am a young black man born and raised throughout South Central Los Angeles, California.

I am the oldest of two children born to my mother and birth father. It wasn't for their lack of trying. Later in life, my mother informed me that she had several miscarriages before I arrived, and even that was touch and go. Initially, I was not breathing when I came out of the womb. My late grandmother informed me that it was prayer that put breath in my lungs. My sister is exactly a year and a half younger than me. My first five years were filled with family, church, and parents who loved me. Despite everything that went on outside the walls of our homes, whether it was San Pedro, Long Beach, or South Central, inside was a safe space. This remained consistent even though my dad was not. He departed the first time when I was around six and would leave the final time when I was about 8. I never saw my mother struggle, and we never saw our refrigerator empty.

A few years later, my mother remarried my father, who raised me. My sister and I were blessed to have a loving, firm, and purpose-driven two-parent household. While there were hiccups with school administrators and local authorities, I was truly blessed to return to a house that expected more of me. That led to me becoming more focused in school and changing my circle of friends. After graduating High School and moving out, I embarked on my adventures as a young black man. My goals were work, travel, and experience until I became an instant father at 24. After 13 years, four more children, and a career change later, I find myself enjoying fatherhood and mentoring the next generation of men.

Purpose Defined

Purpose is someone defining their reason for being. Their reason for waking up in the morning is their purpose. When someone knows their purpose, they are fulfilling the will of God. They're doing what they are tasked to do on this Earth. When you are living, moving, breathing, and operating in what you're destined to do, the world is a better place, you have a better sense of fulfillment and achievement in yourself, and you understand. You know you are fulfilling your purpose.

My Purpose

My purpose for being on this Earth is to be a father and fulfill the fatherhood role of all my children. Really, not just to them, but the young people and kids that have been extended around me that I have brought in my circle and been able to mentor and help, whether that be nieces or nephews or others.

I grew up around several people who did not make the best choices. Wanting to be of service to others, I decided to work in mental health advocacy, similar to how I ended up in my prior career in law enforcement. In the mental health space, I've worked with several nonprofit organizations. I am a facilitator and contributor to Black Men Heal, which helps provide free mental health services for black men because we are often the forgotten-about group. I saw that we were, at times, neglected and left out. Society had overlooked this group of men when it came to mental health, work-life balance, and just overall well-being. So, I'm very proud of participating and engaging with people who look like me to find lost people who are often forgotten in that conversation.

If you're local where I live in Atlanta, you can volunteer at a place called Gateway Center and engage in everything from adults to youth, in mental health, and homelessness. They provide a large realm and scope of services for those underprivileged. Black Men Healing is on all platforms—Twitter, Instagram, and Facebook. They are on every Sunday, a group called King's Corner, that convenes and fellowships, where black men get together and have open, valid, and vulnerable discussions on every topic possible. You should reach out to any of these groups, tap in, and follow and become part of it. It's a great fellowship of men assisting men.

My past work in law enforcement supported my purpose. Similar to the mental health work, I was a youth who was more than troubled. I spent my time having issues with the law. Despite coming from a good home, I still elected to do things on my own that put me in the eyes of law enforcement and some challenging situations. So, from my experience, I realized as a youth that there wasn't enough intervention from law enforcement. It was more of a practice of the iron fist in the policy instead of actual community engagement, stepping out on the front line, being able to reach out and be someone beyond that badge.

So, I fell into the law enforcement career because I knew there needed to be a change concerning people who looked like me. I wanted my position in the community to have a positive impact as opposed to just doing it as a job—to be seen as someone who tried to intervene and mitigate possible future issues with young men who looked like me and had followed a similar path. I felt doing that job and having the authority, just that presence and the uniform, allowed me to be a blessing to so many young men when I would volunteer to show them how where they are now was different from where they had to end up.

What Separated Me from the People I Grew Up With?

The only difference between me and some of my friends growing up was that I had parents who cared for and invested in me. I know at times, often the single-parent home or the two-parent homes can have problems. My suggestion to the young men who may come from troubled homes is to find someone who they can trust, who loves them and has a real genuine interest in their growth and their trajectory in life overall. Find people who will invest in you; you'll feel it within yourself that this is someone who cares for you, not just because you're an athlete or in entertainment, or whatever the avenue is. You will realize for yourself that this is somebody who wants to see you succeed. So, surround yourself with those kinds of people.

Events and Destiny Inform My Purpose

I was destined to be a father. I was destined to advocate for mental health. I was destined to see some things I saw growing up as a kid, which led me to be an interventionist on behalf of young men. But two instances in my life sculpted me into where I am now; the first was my birth father leaving my mother when I was around 4–5 years old. Having that absence, that void did something to me. And then, I think on the flip side, the other moment would be when my mother met my father, the man who raised me, seeing him be a man who provided, protected, and guided me and was very loving and caring to two children that he didn't have to care for, but to this day still does. And, you know, he cares for us as if we were his own. And those two moments in my life shaped the man I am today. It was destined for that to happen. So, I strive to avoid repeating certain things I have seen and to be better than the standards set before me concerning fatherhood, manhood, and even being an everyday employee.

I Call on My Values in the Pursuit of My Purpose

I think my faith as a Christian is one of the most extraordinary things that drive me. If there are any questions that I have, I can find answers in the Bible, the basic instructions before leaving Earth. I will look up every possible devotional concerning fatherhood because, as a father, it's almost as if being anxious and worrying go together. I could always jump into the Good Book and find my needed answer. And I know that it might not be when I get the response, but I know it will reveal itself to me, and it gives me that calming mind that I need to pray daily, and I will continue to press on as a dad when I grow up.

My Contributions

From this Earth, my legacy will be my children who came in, saw what I did, picked up the mantle (saw my accomplishments), and ran laps around the things I did, and my name will carry on in my actions through them. But just because I know we're all designated a certain amount of time on this Earth, there's only so much we can do. So, my prayer is that my kids pick up anything I've done that's positive and just run with it and continue to leave legacy after legacy after legacy of helping people, of being an aid to people, of pulling those up who are downtrodden, and defeated, of being natural change agents. That is my hope and my prayer.

The Impact of My Purposeful Walk

I have been involved with Black Men Heal for around seventeen months, and I have been able to take that information and apply it to being a peer support specialist and well-being champion at Delta Airlines. Even in the short amount of time of meeting with these men, to see them, specifically Black men, who traditionally, regardless of where you are in the diaspora, whether you are Jamaican, Trinidadian, Nigerian, or African American, engaging in conversations we usually don't have because we're forced to be tough and not show emotions.

It has been gratifying and fulfilling to walk into rooms, whether in conversations like Kings Corner, or just in spaces at work and talk with men about fatherhood and vulnerability. And I've seen such immense change among people who look like me. Well, traditionally, those conversations would be bottled up and not let out. So, it's been very, very rewarding to be able to have those talks and to see the subtle change. But even that small change to me has been huge and amazing.

My Collision with My Purpose

I was probably around 14—15 years old, and I remember a minister had come to the church, a prophet, and he said something about my life, "You know, you can change people's lives, and you know, you'll heal people, and you'll change people." And when you're fourteen or fifteen, a young male, living life doing everything, you don't think about it. And one of the things he said to me, and I'll never forget, was "When you speak, people will listen." Over time, I always find myself in places where if it were a crowd of people, the crowd would surround me whenever I spoke. I would say things, and people would listen. I have been in the current role of my job for less than two months now. When I'm in meetings with people who are directors, managers, and international representatives, and I speak, everyone is quiet, and they listen. I'm able to grab their attention. The prophet was correct in what he said about me. I know now that I must have been using my voice to heal people, assist people, aid people, and provide relief to maximize the purpose that I have known I have possessed for over twenty years; there was something in me greater. I didn't know how great it would be.

I Know I Am Walking in My Purpose

I am walking in my purpose when operating in God's will. You are walking in your purpose when doing what you're supposed to do. The road is so smooth; everything transitions so seamlessly. Jobs, family, everything is just in sync, and life is much easier. You don't even look at the troubles and the issues. They're there, but you're driven and focused when moving toward your purpose. The other stuff doesn't even really matter.

Purpose Is Discussed in My Circle

As someone who grew up making many poor decisions, specifically in my youth, I'll use the example of a picture my oldest daughter asks for at least once a year. There is a picture of me and four other young men, these were young men who I had associated myself with for years. And of the five of us in the photo, one has not seen any jail time. Two of them are incarcerated for the remainder of their lives for decisions they made. I look back at that picture and the people I surrounded myself with, even in my youth, and I compare it to those I associate with now.

People are builders who have constructed things and try to elevate those around them. And it's so easy to have those conversations now and be comfortable talking about purpose. What drives you and makes you get up in the morning? It's an amazing experience to have the right people in your circle to where those conversations are just as regular as if you were talking about a football or basketball game.

Finding Purpose

My advice for people, precisely at that young age, is that you don't have to go with the flow. You don't have to follow, even when you're in a leadership role; some people will be leading but still following simultaneously. Many people in that position need to follow what's before them and do the status quo. You can break out of it. You don't have to do what everyone else is doing. If you know that something is wrong in your heart of hearts, if you know it's incorrect, you can break from that and be the friend in your group that causes everyone else to change. For example, I had two friends show up at a party after I graduated from the police academy, and one of them looked at me and said, "They let you be the police! I can't believe it! I mean, you've come a long way, man. I'm proud of you." You can be the change your friends, family, and those around you need. Hearing that from someone I used to run the streets with and hung around warmed my heart.

I'm not going to be "regular." I'm not going to do what everyone else does. I'm going to break stride and go my own way. And if you have that real leadership in you, they will naturally follow you. During one of the funnier conversations with that same friend, he stood there and said, "You?" I said, "Yeah, man." To hear him say, "I'm so proud of you, bro," to hear those words even now, at this moment, thinking of all the things that we did as kids that we shouldn't have done or being in those situations we should have avoided, I am genuinely thankful because, as I said, the difference between myself and my friends is that I had two parents in the home who loved each other and poured in and invested in me. They made sure that I was on the right track. And even when I was on the wrong path, they put me on the right one again. So yeah, those were good times.

When I Am Off the Rail

It was primarily my father who got me right. I know a lot of people in my situation. If it's just a single-parent home, a lot of times, it's the mother. My mother was always there. During the period when she was single, she had to be a little harder on me. But she also surrounded me with good men like my uncles and great-uncles. But my father was, from the time he arrived in my life, always very stern and corrective but would always say something positive on the back end of his chastisement. He always told me, "Look, I'm doing this because I love you, and I do it because I know you will be someone great." So, I always tell fathers to say something positive with the correction. Another thing is my father was always present to ensure I got back in line.

The expectation from him as a father sometimes put me on the path where now, as a father myself, I'm not necessarily angry with my kids, but knowing they have more in them can make me disappointed because I want more for them. Those are the moments where I said I have to do this right.

Purpose Must be a Focus in our Classrooms

Often, we enroll students in the educational system, specifically in public schools, without any emphasis on purpose. Students complete their coursework, and then they go on to get a college degree, but there's still not enough emphasis on purpose. In essence, purpose comes down to each student who is left on their own to pursue and find their purpose. You might have a person who could be an average student across the board, but their brain operates in a way where they function better in mathematics. They might be into coding or science, technology, engineering and math, called STEM, but it doesn't show in the classroom. So, each individual is left on their own to find their purpose.

When you look at statistics, most people who graduate with a primary or secondary degree don't operate in that space, not in the area where they hold a degree. I've worked with people who had master's degrees in chemical and mechanical engineering, biology, and science, and they were working as dockworkers or inspectors for the Transportation Security Administration (TSA). They felt like they were missing out on their purpose. When they were ten or twelve years old, it could have made a lot of difference if someone had taken the time to ask them questions like: What do you want to do? What is it you feel that your purpose is? We do it in elementary school. My daughter will come home every day, and she will say, "You know, Dad, I want to be a doctor and a dancer. I want to be a singer." My second oldest daughter forever wanted to be an astronaut and/or a ballet dancer. And though she'll be in junior high school soon, she still says the same thing.

Talking about purpose has to happen regularly everywhere, specifically with our youth. If teachers take the time to ask kids about their purpose in school, those conversations would be more effortlessly facilitated, even in the home, because it must occur. My purpose was fulfilled.

My Legacy

When it is all said and done, and I am gone from this Earth, I pray I am remembered as someone who was an active father, who was a present father, and whose legacy will be his children loved him so much that they, too, wanted to build upon that of being active and present. Even if they don't have children, they adopt those around them, bring up people, save lives, change how people think, normalize mental health, normalize vulnerability for men, and just be able to help the world. It seems really cliche. I want my legacy to be a good father who taught his children to help others.

My Final Thoughts

My takeaway for the readers would be when you're stirring at night, and you know you can't sleep or are up in the morning, your brain runs, or it's the middle of the day, and you imagine things you don't usually imagine, you're dreaming dreams inconsistent with your job or what you do, most of the time, those things that are stirring, those thoughts that are popping up, that's your purpose. The moments where you're at your job that you work because you have a mortgage and obligations, you're coaching kids, working at the church, feeding the homeless, selling real estate, practicing law, and feeling that smile on your face, that happiness, that joy inside—that's your purpose.

You should work every day to find out what your purpose is. And when you find it, plan what you need to do to achieve that purpose. Put yourself on the right path. But as I said, you don't have to. You don't have to do it. But I have learned through life, God will provide for you, and you won't lack anything. You will have put yourself in a position to learn and follow your purpose. Because when you're operating in your purpose, the world is a much, much better place.

Intentionality, Self-engagement, and Introspection

Intentionality is the keyword to use. You are being genuine. Be real in whatever you are doing. If you're not doing it with real intention, it's fruitless—you're just doing it just to do it instead of coming from a place where you want actual outcomes, where you want real change. So, when you do something, if you're not doing it with intentionality, why are you even doing it? If you're not doing it willingly, there's no need for it to be done.

Stay On Your Purpose

Please find your purpose, operate in it, and get on the path. I would specifically speak to any young men out there to who the algorithm presents itself. Where you are right now is different from where you'll end up. It could look tough right now. This is not the ending. These are the words of the great Nipsey Hussle. "It's a marathon, and the marathon continues every day." Every day is a new opportunity for you to start, for you to grind, for you to get on that purpose. It's not where you are now. To all the dads out there, whether you be the father there every day or the long-distance dad like me doing zooms, stay focused and on purpose. Being a father is a thankless job, but it comes out at the end of just being able to see your child flourishing and succeeding past your level of achievement. It may not look like it now, for all those people, but where you are now differs from where you will end up. Stay focused. Stay on purpose!

Living On Purpose

"Living a fulfilling life for me was more than being educated and financially independent."

Kaye Anderson

Kaye Marie Anderson is a passionate mentor, community outreach strategist, and teacher. After spending over thirty-four years in the healthcare industry as a registered nurse, Kaye retired and committed her time to helping others become their best and most healthy selves through facilitating personal development programs. When not spending time helping and working with others, Kaye can be found enjoying nature, the lake, and family time with her children and husband.

My Early Years

When I think about childhood, there are so many influences that helped to shape my values and my life. Education was always the prevailing, non-negotiating conversation in our household. I was blessed to have both parents who tried to encourage and motivate me and provided reinforcements when we did something positive. For example, if we did well on a test, we would get a treat. This only happened sometimes, which was a great incentive for us. I remembered getting a bike once. Whether this was good or bad, the importance of education was fed into my psyche.

Values and Influences

My influences included seeing my grandmother as an entrepreneur and my mother returning to school after having four children. I cannot discount one of my greatest mentors in grade seven, she was one of my teachers. I only knew her for one year, and she made an invaluable impact on my trajectory in my life.

I grew up in a working-class family. My parents immigrated to Canada when I was nine. I lived with my grandparents in Jamaica for four years before migrating to Canada. I remember having discussions with my grandmother about the path to become successful. We discussed the many distractions and traps along the way. She adamantly warned us to be aware of those traps and to stay away from them. "Focus on putting your head to your book," she would often say. My grandmother and I sometimes would have this imaginary conversation about what I would be when I grew up. It has always been rich and living in a big house.

One of the things that I observed with my grandmother and my parents was the support they sacrificially offered to others. Whether providing a meal to someone or helping someone with temporary shelter. My grandmother mentored many; I learned some of this information at her funeral. And I see similar things in my mother. My sister is a social worker and community advocate; I don't have to wonder where that came from.

A few years later, I went to live with my parents in Canada. My mind was focused on being financially independent and what I thought would come in the way of education, so education was the second thing. By the time I was eleven, I understood to accomplish the things I wanted, I would have to work hard. So, when I got to high school, I had begun to realize the subjects I liked, the ones I had to take, and the ones that challenged my brain. Obviously, I gravitated to the ones I liked and the compulsory ones, I had no options.

Looking at my career path options, I thought, *Can I make a living from doing this? Is there job security in this? Is this a skill I can do anywhere in the world?* These questions helped to form my decision. So, I chose healthcare, although I didn't like hospitals because I thought it was a sad place.

When it was time to apply for college, I went through a process of elimination. For example, again, I looked at what subjects I liked, and from that list, I chose nursing. It could have been anything in health sciences or even social sciences. I didn't grow up wanting to become a nurse; it was a decision I made when I applied to college. So, I feel like I accidentally bumped into nursing. Yet, I can't imagine doing anything else.

I became a nurse and enjoyed the financial independence it afforded me. To me, it was a means to an end, it provided me with the life I dreamed about living as a child, but it was not fulfilling. Twenty-two years into my nursing career, I was bored and was feeling unfulfilled. Your unhappiness and lack of fulfillment from your meaningless 9:00 to 5:00 job will lead you to thinking, *I need another job*. So, you move from job to job, but it is still not gratifying.

Eventually, when you are sick and tired of going to a job that is not rewarding or fulfilling, if you're true to yourself, you will start to explore and think, *There must be something more to life than this!* At this point, you should be true to yourself and take some quiet time to meditate, reflect, and pray.

I was at a crossroad in my life. I had already invested a lot of time and money in my career. Yes, I was making good money, but my job was becoming mundane and burdensome. I was just sick and tired of what I was doing and wanted a change. I asked myself whether I am doing what I'm supposed to be doing. That's what brought me to pursue my purpose.

So, I started a journey that changed my life. I began exploring the process of changing my career. I went on this path intentionally for one year. What I found changed my life. It was like a light bulb went off in my whole being. The questions I was searching for answers to were: What is my purpose? What was I born to do? So, after twenty-two years in my profession, I was grappling with these questions. I wanted to make the right decision. I was married with two children in the university and had a mortgage. I did not want to invest my time and finances into something that would not be fulfilling. It would be a waste. So those questions were birthed into that thought process.

Walking in My Purpose

On my journey, I sought some wise counseling from a mentor of mine. He said, "God does not intend for your purpose to be a mystery. You are probably accomplishing some of it now. The challenge may be determining which aspect of your skills and potential contribution do you want to focus on." These statements torpedoed my direction, and I still have the email and a printed copy of it. I have now learned how to classify such an awareness—it was a Collision With My Purpose.

I did the work that was needed. I zeroed in on the aspect of nursing that I was always drawn into but needed to be made aware of its impact. I started to ask those who know me well to tell me some things about my personality. I made a list of things that came to my mind as well, and I highlighted the topic, "My Purpose." After refining and clarifying over time, I developed this truth, my purpose, into something powerful that speaks to the core of who God made me to be. I spent a lot of quiet moments by the lake and engaging in nature, whether driving through or just sitting listening to the birds, observing their different colors, and looking at the trees with their differently shaped leaves. This calms my mind from all the clutter and helps me reflect better. I did this at least once per week for many years.

There was no need for a career change. Instead, the gate was open, and the awareness was miraculous. I started to live my life on purpose; my career was more fulfilling. In fact, the Vice President of Nursing wanted to shadow me because she had heard so much about how good I was as a nurse. I had won awards for teaching and mentoring nursing students, awards specific to patient care. My goal was never to aspire to obtain these awards; I had just learned I was nominated when I won the awards. I loved what I was doing, and my desire was to always impact the lives of those I was interacting with in a positive manner? I was intentional in improving my life in my career and outside of it. I sought out resources to make me better.

Impact of My Purpose

I began to mentor young people regarding their gifts and talents; it was so easy for me to spot them. One day, I got a voice text from one of my mentees. His call made me feel so good. He was a young man on a student visa in Canada to become a doctor. In our conversation that day, I began to show him how much potential he has and what I saw in him. Later that afternoon, he opened up about all the roadblocks and challenges he had been experiencing in his pursuit to become a doctor. I only saw him three times before he moved out of the province about five years ago. Fast forward to 2022, I got a message from him; here is an excerpt:

"Hi, Kaye, I often think of the things you told me in the past a lot, and some of the resources that you have shared with me, and some of the advice and perspectives. I think I see something in myself now that I didn't see in me before. You were one of those who did. So, I want to say, Thank you."

There is nothing more fulfilling to me than doing things like this, knowing I helped someone.

How to Find Purpose

I observed that what comes naturally or easy for me to do may be challenging for others, so I shouldn't want to become who and what someone else is. I believe our Heavenly Father uniquely makes us. I serve others in different capacities, not only in my career but also in my community. The most challenging part of living on purpose for me is stewarding my time well. Living a fulfilling life for me was more than being educated and financially independent (although necessary); it was how I impacted others around me. I remember saying to myself while pursuing my purpose that when I left this world, I wanted to leave my mark. My intention was not from a place of arrogance but the understanding that when you live in your purpose, you will inarguably impact others. So, I want to encourage others to: Do your homework! Do your research! Do your reflection! Do your meditation! And finally, have your quiet time to take it all in.

How Do You Want to be Remembered?

I want to be remembered for what I was called to do and that I did well, whether serving others through my career as a nurse, mentoring, or just being a good listener, compassionate, and supportive of those in need. And lastly, to find our purpose is God's desire for everyone, and because it is God who is at work in us, both to will and to work for His good pleasure (Philippians 2:13). That is where the journey begins in our pursuit of purpose.

A Promise Made

*"God has a purpose for us all. He helps us to know
what to do and when and how to do it."*

Arthur Hines

Arthur "Art" Hines is a husband, a father, an educator, a caregiver, a real estate agent professional, a business owner, and an advocate for social change.

My Early Years

I am Arthur Hines, born in the Heart of Dixie during the mid-twentieth century. During my early years growing up on a farm in Alabama, my childhood was marked with small cotton farms that became extinct, and my family turned to growing livestock and cash crops. My younger siblings played sports at school, but I developed a love for books and reading. Even now, decades have passed, and I still love books and reading.

My God-given Purpose

We all have a purpose, whether we realize it or not. When we seek God's will for us, we throw ourselves into the river of his will and power for our lives. I believe God brought us to earth to fulfill his assignment for us, and in so doing, we encounter our reason for existence. Our purpose, therefore, is a manifestation of his will for our lives. It is our responsibility to seek and pursue through prayer. People often give up after a few halfhearted efforts and conclude that God cannot be found. The Bible teaches us that if we seek, we shall find. To know God takes belief, faith, focus, and follow-through. Since our destiny in life is so intimately tied to the lives of other people with needs, we must commit to help satisfy the needs of others.

I think it's imperative that we seek our God-given assignments and that we seek to apply it in life, otherwise, we are creating a void in the lives of people who are just sitting out there waiting for us to do what we are purposed to do. God has people who are just waiting for us to step up to the plate and deliver the needed services that we are uniquely called to provide for those in dire need of receiving those services. We should never give up on our efforts to seek God's purpose and ask Him for more wisdom, knowledge, understanding, and patience.

If you were to ask me what is one of my primary goals in life, it is to bring joy and a good quality of life to people who otherwise would be suffering. While operating an assisted living facility, I learned that my heart is inclined to care for elderly people. I would get great joy from delivering a good quality of life and helping to make the consumers happy. I spent over ten years working in the environment where I owned and operated an assisted living facility. It amazed me how much joy I could bring to people just by stepping out and living in my purpose.

A Promise Made Was a Promise Kept

This is my personal testimony of an example of this promise. My mother had ten children and spent all her young adult life taking care of us. Her young friends often wanted her to go out and have fun, but she always said, "Oh, no, I can't; I have to stay home and take care of my children." She was highly dedicated to caring for me and my siblings. She didn't cut any corners when it came to taking care of us. I always noticed and appreciated how much she cared.

I was somewhat sickly during my youth; I had boils on my legs. My mom would take me to the doctor, who didn't know much about treating boils, and the doctor would give me penicillin shots. The boils would go away briefly but then would return. Mom got scared after doing that several times and getting the same results.

One day, she told me, "Arthur, I'm so scared; I don't know what's the matter with you. I hope it is not cancer."

I sensed she was scared, so I, too, got scared.

"I assure you of one thing, I will never leave you alone," she went on to say.

After she reassured me of that, I felt better and was less afraid. Even though I did not say it out loud to her at that time, I did say it in my heart, *Mom, l will never leave you alone either.* Those unspoken words tapped into what led me to one of my family-related purposes in life.

Purpose manifested itself when my mother was much older and was sick. More than sixty years had passed since she spoke those reassuring words to me and when I made my unspoken promise to her. She was over ninety-years old, now; our roles had reversed, and I had started caring for her. It gave me great joy to be there with her, to make her laugh, have a good time, and enjoy a good quality of life together. She thoroughly enjoyed me taking care of her, and mutually I enjoyed doing it.

Where purpose showed up in this example was on her last day of life. We had a wonderful last day together. We did everything that she liked to do. We went to the places where she wanted to go. When we got back home, she sat in her easy chair to rest for a while, and she did. She went to sleep, but she never woke up. It had been many years since I made my unspoken promise to her—*Mom, I will never leave you alone.* After I learned that she had passed, miraculously, my unspoken words of promise to her immediately returned to my memory. This, I believe, was a part of my purpose for being with her on this eventful day as she drew her last breath. I had not thought about that conversation with her for many years, but nevertheless, my unspoken promise to her came to my mind. *Mom, you promised me that you would never leave me alone, and I promised you that I would never leave you alone.* A promise made was a promise kept.

Those events with my mother reminded me that God has a purpose for us all. He helps us to know what to do and when and how to do it.

My role as her caregiver was a part of my purpose for being alive and to spend time with Mom on that day. Remember that we have more than one purpose in life. Therefore, I will never stop seeking. When we stay inclined to do God's will, I believe we will always find that there will be more that he has for us to do. So my goal is to continuously seek what God wants me to do for my life, keep my heart inclined toward him, and keep moving forward to do more of whatever he would have me do.

We Have Not Because We Ask Not

We have not because we ask not (James 4:2). If we don't ask God for his blessings and direction, we don't get all we are supposed to have. God will always fulfill his purpose and will bring his fulfillment to us to enhance the quality of our lives. Remember that through a simple prayer, you can change your future.

Ask, and it shall be given to you (Matthew 7:7). To discover your purpose, I suggest that others do what I do. I constantly seek God's will for my life, and the way I do that is through prayer. Keep prayer and purpose always present in your mind and your heart. "God, what is your will for my life?" You seek, and you shall find; not only do you seek just once, but you should always keep seeking, and you will keep finding.

My Purpose Inform My Behavior

I always enjoyed sitting down and conversing with elderly people when operating the assisted living facility. One day, I was talking with a resident who had come to Atlanta from West Virginia.

She mentioned, "I've never been to the beach in my life."

"You mean you've never been to the beach, ever?" I asked.

"No, I've never been to the beach. I'm from West Virginia, and we don't have very many beaches there."

I said, "I'll tell you what; I guarantee you we will be going to the beach." As a result of that guarantee, I initiated a vacation program for her and the entire facility, all the consumers, and all the staff. And out of that came some of our most beautiful experiences because we got all the family members and consumers involved. We let them know that we will be going on vacation every year from now on, so save your money. It turned out to be a wonderful tradition that everyone involved thoroughly enjoyed.

To help me to have a thorough understanding of my purpose, I believe the shortcut for me is to go directly to the source instead of just trying to figure it out alone; I asked God what he would you have me do? God is ever-present, but he will not physically come down and do the work of giving people a better quality of life by taking them places. Instead, he will put people in place to do that job. So I consider myself a vessel who acts physically on his behalf. He's the creator, so he makes things happen for us and does it through people. I position myself as one of his vessels to carry out his will.

Rarely Do My Friends and I Speak About Purpose

Rarely do my friends and I speak in intentional terms related to purpose, but as we converse, it is obvious that it is ever-present in their minds too. I think we need to be more intentional in speaking about the importance of it. This will cause us to be more proactive in finding what we are called to do in the world. If we talked about purpose more deliberately, we would keep our minds, eyes, and consciousness more open to going about doing God's business. If we do that, we will be more focused on our purpose and more proactive in what we do for our service to others. We will have fewer missed opportunities to execute God's plan for us.

Should Purpose Be Taught in the Classrooms?

There needs to be more effort placed on teaching about purpose in the classroom. That could be a feature that significantly enhances student's learning capacity. If students are introduced to speaking about their purpose, awareness would be brought to the students as to the reason for their existence, how purpose works, and how they can use it in their lives and the lives of others. The impact of students who actively and consciously use their calling to affect and enhance the lives of others could be very beneficial to our society.

Purpose Should First Be Taught at Home

Focusing on our reason for being would be very productive in a classroom, if we initiate teaching and practicing it. However, the home should undoubtedly be the starting point for these discussions. Because we're deliberately speaking about the reasons for our existence and the different nuances of how this affects people's lives, a more prominent place for this discussion is in the classroom. This conversation would bring greater awareness to students who don't think about their destinies. Learning about one's life's journey is essential for everyone, including those students who believe it may come into their consciousness at some point, but right now, they have yet to determine their life's mission. Currently, most students live day to day and never give this aspect of their existence a thought. Studying one's life's mission and helping students discover their life's purpose can be enhanced and, therefore, should be taught in the classroom.

There needs to be more attention regarding teaching about purpose in the home. This deficit typically exists with the child because there may be a deficit with the parent. The deliberate effort of talking about purpose starts with the parent; ensuring they understand its impact on their lives is a prerequisite for helping their children to know why teaching this concept is of the utmost importance.

Let's be mindful that in asking the parent to talk to their child about purpose, the element of making sure that the parent is aware of their own purpose and how it applies to their life personally is very important. This also will be helpful in getting them to start the conversation and spread their informed knowledge among our youth.

I have worked with our youth in the classroom. Even though there is a flaw in the general thinking of us adults, we think our youth are going to hell in a handbasket, and it's an insurmountable problem. No, that thought is wrong. Our youth have a very bright future. Many of them may have a different way of learning and understanding the reason for their existence. But with informed adults showing students the way through teaching them about purpose, we will be amazed at the resulting outcomes. In terms of students learning about their calling, it's our job to help students get the correct information about their life's journey.

I think there is a different kind of spirit that comes through that pulls them away from a wholesome type of belief that leads them in the direction where they should not be going in terms of God's will. At the same time, since today's youth are exposed to much more than many adults were exposed to at their age, their ideas and concepts differ. That is not necessarily a bad thing. Youths are supposed to build on what we have given them, but at the same time, we do have a role to play in helping them within a specific boundary that will deliver them to a better place. If we allow them to be exposed to all kinds of crime and all kinds of killings and sin and those kinds of things, then we need to do anything we can to help offset that. That's the best justification for what we must do, as in teaching them about purpose. We all agree that responsibility must be shared between them and us.

To avoid a generation of the perpetuation of what is not necessarily the appropriate approach to pursuing their purpose, we must go back to the source because, ultimately, in discussing our destiny, we must go back to our beginning. When we discover who we are it goes beyond something that pops into our heads or happens to come to mind. Our life's journey was designed and laid out continuously by our creator since we were born, and it is our job and responsibility to seek that purpose. If you seek to find the reason for your existence, then you shall find it—you will find it through prayer.

Error in Our Thinking About Finding Purpose

Failure of some individuals to find meaning in their lives starts with a lack of knowledge. Many erroneously think *I don't need a purpose as my priority because it may come automatically someday. Or perhaps if I want to delve into my purpose, I will think of something I want to do and simply do it.* These thoughts represent errors in our thinking. It would be better for people to understand that to know their purpose, they need to seek it. They don't need to leave it to chance. They should seek and find the reason for their existence correctly. Then, they can better spread that knowledge to their children and others as they pursue their destiny. Properly teaching purpose is an approach that can be more effective because the learner can hear you say it and see you living it before adopting your method as their own. Therefore, that is a more practical approach to advancing God's will in our lives and serving our purpose in the world.

Intentionality and Purpose

Intentionality and purpose enhance our use of and indulgence in our lives. They work hand in hand, like man and wife. We should do it deliberately if we desire to live a meaningful life and deliver goods and services to others. We will also be more effective and efficient at it.

It is said that if you have a destination, you can use a map to help you get to where you are going. If you get in your car with the intention of going somewhere but don't have any specific directions or destination, you won't know where you will end up. It could be in Miami, or you could find yourself in New York. Intentionality, however, is more practical and efficient at getting us to our desired destination—our Purpose. You are not just aimlessly driving around. When you are determined and have a destination that gives you a definitive target, you will not wander. Therefore, we should always be intentional in seeking God's will for our life.

Are You Operating in Your Purpose?

Knowing when you're operating in your purpose is important. Sometimes, miracles occur in our lives to confirm our calling. When I see miracles related to certain things in my life, I do not doubt that I am operating in my purpose. Miracles are often tied to purpose because they give you an example or illustrate how God is always intimately involved in our daily lives. He knows exactly what we are doing and where and why we are doing it. God will miraculously use his supernatural power to give you the resources to help us when needed.

When my mom needed a new lawnmower, I called Walmart to find out how much it would cost to buy the new lawnmower for her. There was one that I thought I could buy, but it cost $387. When I checked my account, it had less than $300 in it. I was about $100 short of what I needed to complete the purchase. I thought, *Today is just Saturday, and it will be Tuesday before I had more money added to that account to make that purchase. I really don't want to wait until Tuesday to make the purchase because I want to cut the grass this weekend.*

Years ago, you could float a check and maybe get by for a couple of days before it cleared, but these days, you can't do that. Withdrawals from your account are almost instantaneous. I thought there must be some way to make this purchase today because today is Saturday, and Tuesday is several days away. Those are the facts, but I decided to try it anyway. What happened is that I got my mom ready and put her in the car so we could drive to Walmart to purchase the lawnmower.

We had gone a short distance when I decided to return to the house to ensure all the lights were out. When I went to my room, all the lights were indeed turned off, but, lo and behold, there was a miracle staring me in my face. On the bed I had just made up a few minutes earlier, was a big pile of money with bills of different denominations. It was so much money that I didn't have time to count it, because I had left my mom in the car, and I was concerned it might get too hot. So, I decided to take the $100 bill that I would need to complete the purchase at Walmart and deal with counting the rest of the money when we returned.

This was mind-boggling because I had just made that bed, and it had no money on it, but now that bed was full of money. When I came back home, all that money was not there any longer; it was all gone. The $100 I got for the lawnmower was good, spendable money that I used at Walmart to purchase the lawn mower. That was the day I learned that miracles are real, and God as our "on-time God" is real. God is intimately tied to what we do and how we do it daily. The money was something that I didn't think to ask Him for, but he certainly miraculously provided it for me.

Be A Believer in the Power of God, Not A Knower

We must be believers, not knowers. GOD gives us no credit for knowing but only for believing in his omnipotent power. I do, however, believe to the point of knowing the illustration that we just talked about helped my belief to reach that level. It helped my belief to the point of knowing because before that experience, if someone had said to me, "I don't think there is any such thing as a miracle," I would have responded, "You have a right to consider whatever you please." But now, my belief in miracles has evolved tremendously, and I am more likely to say to that person, "I truly believe you could benefit from hearing about my encounter with miracles. God has shown me that miracles do happen. I cannot say that I know, but I do believe to the point of knowing that miracles are real."

I Have Substance

"There's just something about acknowledging with each breath that I have substance and this amazing thing to contribute to life."

Romaine McNeil

Miss Romaine McNeil is a visual artist and the CEO and owner of Romaine Creates. Her paintings explore the ever-evolving changes in personal and societal identity.

My Early Years

During my early years, I was a quiet child. I was a loner. I've always been a loner. I'm a deep thinker. I am always thinking about something. I'm constantly questioning things and analyzing things. My childhood experiences paved the way for how I view life and approach living. As a child, I've always had this way of just absorbing. That's the word I want to use, to absorb my surrounding environment and people's energy. And I grew up hoping to learn from my surroundings and learn from how people function and how life is, in general. That was what grounded me as a child. I grew up in Grange

Hill, Westmoreland, Jamaica. Both my parents were teachers. My dad was a principal. And people would always say that teachers' children are unruly and bad, because they spend hours dealing with other people's children, so they don't have the energy to tend to their own kids. But that's not true. I grew up in a space where I was always allowed to be myself and be creative. Growing up as a child, I was always doing something—always active. I played volleyball, football, and tennis.

What is Purpose?

Purpose is how we focus our intention, which is not just one thing. It is not a stagnant word but very fluid, and your purpose will also change as you grow and change. But an individual's core is to be happy with just the basic things. That is the goal! You know, this is what we set out to achieve for ourselves: simply joy and happiness. You know, you're happy when you have that cemented purpose and find balance in everything. The happier you are, the more you can see life the way it is when material things do not cloud your mind, and you're not confused by stress or the heaviness of what the world is trying to throw at you.

Importance of Purpose

Knowing and understanding your purpose is crucial because absent that knowledge, you would spiral out of control. You would be pulled in every direction, and when you're drawn in every direction, you begin to lose yourself; you don't know who you are, and it's important to at least have an idea of who you are. And in having an idea, you must understand what you are destined to do and the importance of your existence.

Talking about my reason for being brings me back to the purpose of creating. For me, the essential pursuit is happiness. I derive joy from the act of creation, which transcends visual art or painting and encompasses the realm of making music. Engaging in creative endeavors is a way to rejuvenate oneself. Through my artistic expressions, I aim to inspire clarity and openness in others, allowing them to engage with their serene energy, whether admiring my artwork or immersing themselves in my music. I hope this experience can guide them towards uncovering their purpose.

Others can find meaning in my work because when I'm creating, it's very cathartic; it releases heaviness and energy and reminds me of why I'm doing it. I'm reminded that happiness and balance are important. When I create the work, people can have a sense of what's important to them because everybody's interpretation will differ. I never want to say, well, this is a painting, and this is the meaning. I am not just creating for me; I'm creating so that other people can see whatever good energy they gain from it. I wouldn't feel right painting something and then just keeping it to myself, because then it's going against my core beliefs I don't want to do that because it's important to share this work. Why? Because sharing the message and work is important because it will help somebody else.

Dr. Stephenson referenced a piece of art called *The Nest*. It is one of two complementary pieces I did at a time when I became a little more reserved than I usually am. I was losing my sense of purpose because

I had just moved back to Kingston and was disoriented and thrown off track, being pulled in different directions, trying to find what it is that I was able to do. I started to create this art piece, a fetus nestled in the earth. I needed to settle and grow myself back into the environment and nature to redefine myself. This piece reminds me that whatever it is that I'm experiencing and whatever it is that someone else is going through, you can always go to a place of centeredness or groundedness. You can redefine what it is that you're supposed to do by identifying your intention, and that will help you get past whatever blocks or hurdles you might be encountering.

My Brand

Romaine Creates is my brand. I didn't want to use my name. I wanted to create a brand where I would start with paintings, but eventually, I branched out with music and photography. Everything will fall under my brand, whether it's music, changes in words, photography, or cinematography. I decided to create a brand that could represent that. So, Romaine Creates is what came to mind.

Interestingly, I like having people come to my studio because it is never about just coming to look at work. It's always a long conversation that comes with the visit, and I really enjoy it because then you get people to open up by just looking at a simple painting, they begin to open up about other things and tell you what's going on in their lives. It is interesting that a painting can allow you to express feelings without judgment. This brings me back to why purpose must remain for me. The core goal is happiness. Once you come to my studio, my painting will help you reconnect with your happiness. That intention is set for me, and it's just such a pleasure and a joy to see people be able to do that by just looking at the artwork.

What Informs My Purpose

My reason for being is informed by part destiny and part of everything else. There is a growing need for support, and with purpose comes support. There needs to be a place you can go to that will help you realize your reason for your existence and intention regarding your goals. Sometimes, if you try to do things alone, it doesn't help. Knowing there will be an impact by what I create, knowing that it will connect with somebody who needs to hear this message, see it, or feel what they need to think from the painting is gratifying. I know that I was given this gift that fulfilled a calling. The amazing part is both my parents allowed me the freedom to create. My dad was quite an artist but he didn't pursue art at all. My mother got me started on piano lessons. Yet, they both nurtured my need to create. For that, I'm very thankful.

Connecting the Dots with Your Purpose

You need that oneness with yourself, which is universal under the broadest spectrum. And once you understand the connection with you, you will understand that people are just different versions of you. It is just a mirror; if you understand they are hurting, you shouldn't judge because it will affect you. After all, you can also hurt; the person next to you can be hurt. This is like a chain reaction of things. If you can find it within yourself to help someone, you're helping yourself, whether it's purpose-wise or just for them to grow and see what they need to achieve in life.

Sometimes when you're helping someone to achieve goals, you think, *I needed to do this for myself. I needed to do this, because I, too, needed to tap into something that would help me to grow and help me to fulfill my purpose.*

We can't be selfish with ourselves because then it breaks down the oneness and connectivity in the world. When this breaks down, imbalance starts to happen, and disease occurs within us. To move past that, we must go back to the root of oneness and connectivity because it's essential. We're all created from one being. We all must stay as one; even though we're different individuals, we are still one. Selfishness takes away from what you are called to do. When you dwell more on selfishness, it takes away from the universal purpose—our intention of how we should be living. We don't want that to occur because that throws off the overall balance of our existence.

There will always be chaos and mayhem if we continue this route, not knowing what we want to achieve. Again, we're pulled in different directions, and we're constantly evolving. We must change, but with purpose. Knowing where you go and what you want to achieve is essential. We must be so intentional about our actions. Because if you're not, you will always be spiraling, going left, right, center, up, or down. When you go into that dark space, then you lose sight of what is important, and you lose sight of what you should be doing. You'll be confused, like a death of the unknown. Again, you must understand what you're doing here, that's for the benefit of everyone. We're all searching, nobody has a definite answer to it. It is all a part of life, it's part of us. But at least we can make it so that we have an idea, because it's important to start somewhere.

What Would Happen If We Lived in a Perfect World

In a perfect world, it would be blissful. I also suspect there would be some calm, and we're here to exist without flaws and problems. That is not the case at all. We're here for the experience of being here, to understand the different stages of our existence and how we can function at each one. And if you're stuck in one space, you'll miss out on all the other phases you could enjoy because you need to work towards your intention, the process takes time.

We should not compare where we are in this process to where someone else is, because they must function at their own distinct tiers. Occasionally, you may see someone struggling. Don't sit back and watch! You can help them to understand the process because you've been there and made it through that particular situation. Everybody is equipped mentally, emotionally, and psychologically, but to varying degrees. No one should look down on anyone else and say, "Well, that's stupid, why are you behaving like that?" Instead help them.

My Values and Beliefs

My values are oneness and understanding that we're all here and exist in this space. I practice selflessness every day while painting, thinking about how to be more selfless. Can I contribute more to society? How can I lend a listening ear to someone? It doesn't have to be of any significant value. It doesn't have to be from a monumental place, it could be as small as a text message saying, "Hey, I'm just checking on you. Are you okay?" My values are always coming from a place of love.

My intentions always come from a place of love, caring, understanding, and being non-judgmental. Once we understand that people have different values, we should respect them and not infringe or try to push our set of values onto them. Again, we're all experiencing life differently. And yeah, it's important to know that to hold your own values are important. Don't change because of someone else. Hold onto your values of love, selflessness, understanding, non-judgmental, and openness—open to caring, and being human.

Unique Contributions to Humanity & The Fulfilment of Your Purpose

Understandably, it is challenging that your purpose is a drop among billions of people. But if your purpose can vibrate so strongly, it will cause a ripple effect that would help others in humanity to vibrate just as strongly. Part of that is understanding that the human body is made up of matter and energy; so, we're all energies, we're all frequency. Each of us occupies a frame in life and has a responsibility, a job, and a purpose. We can unite, cultivate understanding and love through the connections we establish as humans, and pursue a balanced, harmonious existence and a valuable life. Achieving this is less complex than it might seem. It doesn't take a lot to do this. Many people overthink it—I don't have this, or I don't have that. But, you have life, breath, and the ability to share kind words that you can say. I give as much as I can.

Understanding who I am is one of the most important things during my journey while still being grounded in my purpose. It takes a lot of work. Through the years, I've changed, but my core purpose remains the same—I want to be happy, if I am happy, then I can contribute happiness to the world in a broader range. It's not just in my space. It is not just toward my friends. I can share words of encouragement to everyone because I am happy. When you're sad, it's different. It's heavy, and a dark force or energy surrounds you. You can only fulfill your vision for your life if you have good energy. When you don't, you can't; you can't see a way out. My core belief is always to be happy, to find happiness, and spread joy.

Walking in My Purpose

Sometimes, it is challenging because I don't always feel like I'm up to being happy or creative. People tell me you have found your purpose. You create great art, beautiful art, and make music. And the truth is, you won't always feel that way. You won't always be like that and want to go down that road every day. It's just impossible, you know? But again, I'm happy whether I am doing this extension of my core purpose or whether I get up and paint. If I get up and write, I'm good because that will lead to me thinking about tomorrow or having a better conversation with somebody else two days after that. It's always challenging to follow a path, and no formula will help you to be great at it. You learn along the way, and you adjust while you're traveling. And do the best you can.

Advising Individuals Facing Challenges with Finding Purpose

The first thing I would ask someone is, What makes you happy? Regardless of what else is going on in your life, what puts a smile on your face, even if it's not a very wide smile, but it lightens your mood and how you feel about yourself? When you can answer that, then you can begin to narrow down one or two things. For me, purpose isn't just one thing. It's a combination of many things. If you can narrow down what works for you, then that is how you can see the path to find your reason for existence.

How Do You Want to be Remembered?

I want to be remembered as someone that walks the truth, who knew what they wanted to be. I said what I was going to say; I did what I was going to do. When I was around eight years old, I was asked what I wanted to do as a profession. I said, "I want to be an artist." At fourteen, I was asked that same question again, and said, "Well, I want to be an artist." At eighteen, I was asked the question again, and the answer stayed the same. So yeah, I want to be remembered as someone who knew what they wanted and went after it and did it with such purity and joy.

My Reflection About My Parents and My Purpose

Before my father passed, he was always supportive. He bought my first painting when I was fourteen. I did a nice landscape. He bought it and put it in his office so everybody could see. And he was just so proud. However, my mom grew to appreciate what I did at a later stage, when I was in my thirties. There was one painting she saw, and the first thing she said to me is, "It's something that you created. It moves something inside of me." In that moment, she realized how much I loved and enjoyed what I did. Every time there was something written about my work, she saved it; if there is a TV interview, she is so proud. My family has always been so supportive of what I have done and still are. And for me, there is no retirement.

Is Purpose a Common Discussion in Your Circle of Friends

Maybe not to the degree that I think about it, but to the degree they wonder why they're still here. I have this amazing job and am doing things that matter to me. Because you have people out there who don't feel that need, they don't think they need to be here anymore. When I discuss with my friends what is important to them during this life, they will often talk about the things that keep us grounded, the things that keep us happy—the community, the connections, and the conversations. It's like simple things. It's not going out and partying, and it's not going after something that may fade after a while. It is deeply rooted in our beliefs that there is a greater purpose for everybody, not just getting up in the mornings and drinking coffee and going to work.

You will be aligned to do other things when called upon to do them. Do you know what I mean? We'll talk about stuff like that and about the greater good, and not being selfish. Not selfish wisdom, not being selfish with anything. We are trying to find a place to contribute to the greater good.

My Music

But music, for me, is more therapeutic. It is more of an internal dialogue; it's where I retreat to re-energize myself. Sometimes you get this vibe and start feeling at ease when playing. You're so focused, you're so present, you're so here, and it removes some of the clutter, distortion, and noise you're surrounded by. When I sit around my keyboard and play, it's just me and the keyboard. At that moment, work does not exist. If I take out my guitar and practice, it is just me. I am just there. I am present with myself, love myself, and think it's all about music for me.

Because we grew up constantly hearing negative things, even if it wasn't intentionally meant to be negative, creating music became more of an introspection, like things that I need to do, to fix, tend to, whatever scars or damages that were done, even by myself.

For me, being an artist, you're a loner. People don't understand you. It's not like you're a weird person, but people may wonder why you sit in the corner with your sketchbook. Music, for me, helps to languish that pain and suffering. And it just re-energizes me. I like that. I want to be in a space with nothing else. Just me and the music. Even when I'm drawing, I want to paint. And it's a way for me to improve what I do. I am not thinking about many other things. The night doesn't get to where you are just alone with what you do; you're alone with your life's work. The purpose is to be happy. I am alone with this energy to be satisfied at that moment. I don't have to deal with the world. I don't have to deal with my dogs, and I don't have to deal with driving out on the road. I'm just there, and happy.

Who Checks You?

My partner puts me in check, and I have checked myself. I don't have a lot of friends. Those closest to me know when I need them without ever having to say, "Hey, I need a shoulder." I'm also an animal lover and enjoy being in the space with my dogs. Dog lovers probably understand this way more than people who do not have pets, but they sense things. I've had instances where I was painting for hours on end, just sitting there. I was so involved in my work, and it was becoming so emotionally heavy that my dog picked up on it, and she would come, sit, and tap me. And then I'd come out of my zone and say, "Oh, what time is it?"

So to know your circle is key because I will have people who, if I go missing, and when I say missing, I mean if I go in my space for a couple of days, they will ask, "Romaine, are you okay?" They check on me, because they know when I get in that zone of work, I might not know how to get out, you know? I have an excellent support system. I have amazing friends that are always there.

My Final Words

Believe in yourself. Don't let anyone say that you don't have a purpose. Don't let anyone say that you're nothing. Don't let anyone tell you that you're not worth anything. Don't let anyone tell you those things because you *are* here for a reason. When you figure that reason out, it will be one of the most liberating experiences you will ever have. So, to anyone out there who is struggling, know that you are here for a reason. Because if you're not, you wouldn't be here. You're still here; you're still breathing. There's just something about acknowledging with each breath that I have substance and this amazing thing to contribute to life. Don't let anyone tell you that you're not worth it. Don't let anyone tell you that you can't achieve anything, and you shouldn't set goals because you are worthless. For it is not true! You are not worthless.

We are all a puzzle; we fit somewhere, and puzzles cannot be completed if you take yourself out completely. You are a part of the puzzle. Therefore, you do have a purpose for the story to be complete. For the picture to be whole, you must fit. You must know and understand that you serve a purpose. Some have discovered, and some are still discovering. Take your time because there is no rush. You shouldn't be in a hurry because you recognize that your friends probably figured out their purpose, and you're still not there yet. There's no rush. You have years; believe that you will find your purpose. Everybody goes through things, but in our imperfections, we can still find joy. We can still have understanding, and we can still be loved and feel love. Take the time to get to know you. Take the time to learn who you are and to discover what you're here to do.

SECTION III

Crashing Into Purpose

Crashing into Purpose is an exhilarating, sometimes chaotic, but ultimately transformative journey. It is the experience of colliding headfirst into a profound sense of direction and meaning when life is in disarray. Often, it begins with unexpected events or circumstances that disrupt the status quo, leaving you feeling disoriented and vulnerable. Amid this chaos, there's a powerful awakening. People start questioning their choices, desires, and values, seeking clarity amid the wreckage.

Crashing into Purpose is a process of self-discovery, a journey into the depths of one's passions, talents, and aspirations. As the pieces of life's puzzle fall into place, a newfound purpose emerges from the wreckage, illuminating the path forward. This Collision With Purpose can be both invigorating and daunting, demanding courage and a willingness to embrace change. Yet, in these moments of impact and transformation, people often find their most authentic selves and a profound sense of fulfillment, forging ahead on a path that resonates with their true calling.

Dr. Laxley W. Stephenson

I've Lost It All

"I've achieved everything they said I'm supposed to achieve, and now I've lost it all, what else is there?"

Lexi Johnson

Lexi Johnson is a servant of God, wife, and mother with a mission to help female entrepreneurs master their money so they can advance the kingdom of God.

My Early Years

I was born to Samuel and Juanita, immigrants from Honduras, Central America. They came to the United States as teenagers and settled in New York, where they married and conceived me. With a baby on the way, my nineteen-year-old father needed a good job. My great aunt influenced him to work as a steelworker in East Chicago, Indiana.

While my father worked, my mother stayed home for the first few years of my life. She started a pre-school called Apple Day Nursery in the basement of our home. I and a few other neighborhood kids were her first students. This is where the seed of entrepreneurship was sown into my being.

I am the oldest of three, with one sister and one brother. As far back as I can remember, we went to church every Sunday. I was raised Lutheran. Our at-home nightly devotion, led by my mother, almost always occurred every night. I don't recall her missing devotion, not even if we traveled. To this day, she reads her Bible every night at the same time. Each morning, my siblings and I were required to read our daily devotion from a book called "Keys for Kids," which still exists today!

By the time I was nine years old, my parents divorced. I witnessed my mother teaching herself how to drive, handle household finances, and more. My mother constantly told us that we did not have to go to college, but we needed to get a trade, a certification, or something. Because of her experience with my father, she taught us to be God-fearing and independent. My father taught me and my siblings work ethic. He did not miss work. The only time that I recall my father not going to work was when he had surgery.

Purpose Defined

I am a woman of faith. My faith is at the center of everything I say and do. For me, purpose starts with finding your "why." Why did God put you on this earth? That is your purpose. Let me put it this way. If you create something, you invent that thing for a specific purpose. You mold that thing and shape it. You put it out there in the world for it to work. You are excited and happiest if the thing you created is doing what you purposed it to do. You think, *Ahh, success!* It is the same for us as humans—God's creation. As believers, we believe God is our maker, our creator. He has put each one of us on this earth for a specific purpose. God rejoices when each one of us is walking in what we were designed and created to do.

Purpose vs. A Calling

I believe this is an area where many of us are confused and seeking clarity. This is because of the way we are conditioned. We are conditioned to seek out what we will do instead of focusing on who we are to become. Because of our conditioning, we think that our purpose is all these various roles that we may have or jobs that we have. We might think, *Oh, my purpose is to be a mom, my purpose is to be a nurse, or my purpose is to be a basketball player.* Purpose is more general than all these specific roles. For example, you know, your purpose may be to transform or inspire, motivate, or encourage, or advocate.

Though purpose and calling are used interchangeably, calling is distinctly different. A call answers the question of how I present my purpose to the world.

My Purpose

My purpose is to transform lives. How do I do it? I can do it in a multiplicity of ways. I choose to do it by helping people, particularly women entrepreneurs, with their money and helping them create wealth, make a Kingdom impact, and leave a legacy of wealth. That's my calling. I believe, as people get clear on what purpose is and what it's not, then we'll find more people walking in their purpose.

What Informs Purpose?

It is a combination of things. It can be a series of events. It can be, for those of us who are Believers, predestined. We're not forced, but we are predestined. Meaning it's here for us if we choose. In my experience, what has informed my purpose are life events, my passions, my personality, and my spiritual gifts. Those are the main things that have informed me as to what my purpose is.

From Pain to Purpose

The light bulb came on when I was going through a significant amount of pain, a series of traumatic events. Between 2008–2011, just about anything negative that you can imagine happened to me—from bankruptcy to divorce, repossessions, and foreclosure. I became a single mom of three small children and experienced a short stint of homelessness. These events jolted me into asking myself, *What am I doing? Why am I on this earth? What's going on? What am I going to do?*

When I would reflect on my life, I thought I did everything right. I went to school and got my degree. I had this great paying job; I was married; I had the house with the white picket fence, the two and a half kids, and the pet. Well, I had to have a fish because I'm allergic to dogs and cats. For the most part, I did what I was supposed to do or what society said I should do to live a purposeful life and be happy. For all of that to come crashing down during that three-year period, I just couldn't understand.

The weight of these devastating events caused me to feel like this must be the end. If I have achieved everything they said I am supposed to achieve, but now I have lost it all, what else is there? These events eventually sent me on a journey of knowing God better and deeper.

Because I came to know God in a more profound way, I was then able to know myself in a more insightful way. I was able to understand exactly why God put me on this earth.

Oftentimes, the crazy, hurtful, shameful things that have happened to us are the things we want to bury. Ironically, those are the very things that are necessary for you to walk in your purpose and for you to have the impact that you are going to have on the people that you're going to come across.

There was this pivotal moment when I moved into an apartment with my children. We did not have furniture—we didn't have anything. But we had a place to stay. One night, after putting them to bed, I fell to the floor and just began crying that ugly, gut-wrenching cry where you can't even see out of your eyes. You are snotting all over the place, and you don't even care if anybody sees you. Amid that ugly cry—not audibly, but in my mind, because I couldn't even speak—I asked the Lord, why am I here? Can we just end this now? That's where I was. I fell asleep that night lying prostrate on the living room floor.

When I woke up the next morning, I just heard the Spirit say, "Get up." I could have ignored that message and continued to wallow in the pain.

Or I could get up as the Spirit was telling me. So, in that moment, I made the decision to get up and take the first step of faith forward, trusting God to lead me wherever He wanted to lead me.

When you say *yes* to God, *yes* to being in the kingdom of God, your purpose is all about winning souls and making disciples. The way we go about doing that is by serving Yeshua as our master teacher and our example. He was the influential servant of them all. He masterfully walked in his purpose. The Word tells us that we are to serve. We should not look to be served, but we are to serve. And so, every day when I get up, I ask, *Who can I serve today? How can I serve them today?* The Bible says if we are about God's business, we are seeking Him and his righteousness; everything else will be added unto us. So first and foremost, I am a servant of God. I don't lead with all those titles all the time. I am just the average person, like anybody else, trying to live a Godly life.

Living With Purpose

Because of the financial devastation I experienced, one of the areas that I am very passionate about is finances. I told myself I would never be in that situation again, and I would do whatever I could to assist people to either prevent such situations or help them come out of them. Serving in finance brings me great joy. Yes, I help women entrepreneurs, specifically, but whoever God sends my way, I help. I want to train people on how to understand money the way God sees money. I want to help them understand why God gives us money. He gives us money just like he gives us any other resource to further his kingdom.

It is crucial for me to help women to become financially free so they can continue to impact the kingdom of God and leave a legacy of wealth— just as God calls us to do. If we are walking in our purpose and doing what we're called to do, God's going to fund it, right? He's going to make sure that you are taken care of because you're seeking his kingdom first.

I have the awesome and humbling opportunity to lead a mission trip. I have been leading short-term international mission trips for approximately five years. And this year, we are going to Kenya, and we're going to be serving in Kitale and Mombasa. We have a team of fifteen missionaries. They are from different places throughout the United States. Some of our main projects in Kitale, Kenya, include providing footwear—we're calling it Crocs and Sock because we are providing shoes in the form of Crocs to many of the people there. We are going to provide school supplies and sanitary napkins for the young women. Our mission is to provide funds to help Gospel Praise Church in Mombasa, Kenya, put in infrastructure in a village in Mombasa, and I thank God for allowing me to be part of it.

Driven to Serve

Salvation is a gift. My work is an expression of my gratitude to Him for saving me. So, I am just excited about all that God is doing. I am humbled that he is winning with peoples' finances. I can go on and on with a lot of the things that I value. These values drive me to do what I am doing. I feel every person is needed, and this is why I'm so passionate about helping people to understand their purpose.

Oftentimes, people don't tie purpose and create wealth together. But they do work together. Consequently, I want every person to know that they are needed.

My unique contribution comes from this space of helping people get financially free so they can focus on the things of God. What I hear when people come to me is, "I would like to do more of this, but I can't because I don't have the money." I advise people on how to get *free* so there's no excuse as to why they are not doing what God has destined them to do.

The Impact of Living on Purpose

I give credit to God. I try to be a willing vessel in the way that I approach finances and when I'm dealing with my clients. I had a client who once said, "Not only do you get your financial life straight, but you can get your spiritual life straight too."

Faith is central, and I want people to know the truth about God and money; it changes people significantly. They do draw closer to Christ. They do start to see success in their finances when they apply those godly principles and manage their resources in a way that glorifies God. Those resources include money. That impact is priceless. The transformation is priceless. To watch people make those changes in their mindset first and then in the behaviors that follow is everything to me.

The P's of Purpose

Passion. I know I am living my purpose because of the passion I have for my work. It is not fleeting. It is not something that is here one day and gone the next. It is steadfast.

Peace. The next is peace. There is peace in my life. That doesn't mean that things are always going well because they are not. But in the midst of it all, there is still this peace, God's peace. No matter what is going on, there is still this desire every morning to get up and do what I do.

Provision. I know that when I am walking in my purpose, God makes provision. If it is the mission trip that I'm leading, if it is a conference or something I want to put on, or some kind of service I want to do with the community, God will fund it because I am walking in my purpose. God will not sabotage his work.

Possibilities. When you are walking in your purpose, there are so many possibilities. There are doors that begin to open. The opportunities often come from the most unexpected places.

Player Haters. When you begin to have haters, people who are jealous of your walk will criticize you because they also have issues. That, too, can be a sign that you're walking in your purpose.

Partners. God begins to move people, places, and things to make sure that your work can be carried out and that you can fulfill your purpose.

Advice For Those Discovering Their Purpose

Go to your creator and ask Him what you are purposed to do. What were you designed to do? What are you created for? Wait for the answer. He will answer. Oftentimes we are looking for our purpose outside of us, but it is within us. Before God even fashioned us in our mothers' wombs, he knew what we would be created for and what he wanted us to do. We came here with it. Our conditioning along the way suppresses it.

Staying Accountable

The Holy Spirit keeps me in check. Next, my mom, always. My husband and children also hold me accountable. Children have a way of checking you for real. You can't teach them something and then do something different. They will check you. I've learned to allow that checking.

A Legacy of Purpose

I simply want to be remembered as a woman who served God, and as a result of serving God, I hope people will say, "She transformed many lives because God first transformed her life."

Takeaway

You live your happiest and your best life when you are walking in your purpose, period. If you're doing anything outside of it, you are always going to feel emptiness. You will feel unfulfilled, as if you have not realized your full potential. If you're feeling that way, it is time for you to dig in and say, *Okay, what is my purpose, and how do I begin living it?* Let me begin living it. When everyone is walking in their purpose, every need on this earth is met. If you are reading this, you need to walk in your purpose. There are people that you are going to impact because you're walking in your purpose. As a result, your life will also be transformed.

Educate, Equip, And Empower

"I am here to Educate, Equip, and Empower."

Juan Smith

Juan Smith is the Founder of MproveU Coaching & Consulting, LLC, a for-profit strategist company. He has a Bachelor of Psychology from Georgia State University and a Master of Leadership and Administration from Beulah Heights University. In his role as an Independent College & Career Coach, Juan has been committed to guiding young men and women in discovering their God-given purpose. This commitment has also extended to his coaching and consulting firm, MproveU (MpU), established in 2010 under his parent company, Juan Smith Enterprise Companies (Jsent Cos.). He also launched Boarding Pass Travel Group, another JSent Company that enriches lives by cultivating unforgettable travel experiences.

My Early Years

I was born right before the summer of 1983 in Tulsa, Oklahoma. My Mom had just turned twenty, while my Dad was still nineteen. They were both in college. My Dad was a well-known and heavily awarded athlete. My Mom was a cheer and dance team captain and top in her graduating class. As teenage parents, they still managed to push through and graduate on time. In 1986, shortly after they graduated, they decided to get married and move from Tulsa, Oklahoma, to Atlanta, Georgia. Neither of my parents had close relationships with their dads or moms. They were fourteen hours from home, trying their best to build a life for themselves, their four-year-old son, and unborn child.

Growing up, my parents worked a lot to make ends meet, but they ensured that my brother and I had a good education, shelter, clothes, and family. They taught us that family is all you have, so do your best to stay close and love your family. Despite the constant fighting between my parents, my dad's infidelity, his volatile moods and frequent absence, I had a good upbringing.

Now, I am a Certified Master Life Strategist Coach. So, many of the conversations I have every day are centered around discovery—self-discovery, life discovery, careers, family, life in general, coaching people, and helping them find what their pathway looks like.

When I think about legacy and purpose, the most powerful word that comes to mind is alignment. Being in Purpose connects individuals with their calling, even having to think through, "Why am I here?"

Purpose Defined

It's essential to understand why something or someone exists and what they're destined to do; you don't want to spend your whole life walking aimlessly. We often find ourselves wandering because we don't know why we're here. Then the minute it clicks, we are in tune with our existence. Everything starts to make sense—the relationships, the experiences, good, bad, or indifferent. But everything plays into why we exist because it puts us closer to the alignment of our Purpose. I think it's important to know God's will for your life, so we're not just wandering through life. But I believe there is a beauty in the process of figuring it out because then you're able to find yourself—that's the first step to finding you.

Finding You

There are some questions that one should ask themselves to figure out in order to bring clarity to curiosity. You're seeing everything about you, what you love, what you like, all those things, because part of your Purpose is tied to who you are at your core. So, even when you're in that wandering period, there is some self-discovery as you ask yourself, "I can't stay here forever, so how do I get out? Where am I going?" You find the answer; you find direction.

Understanding Your Purpose

Legacy is vital because when we fulfill our Purpose, it transcends our lifetime. Generations to come will be informed by what we do, what we figure out, and share during our lifespan.

I Know My Purpose

My Purpose is to Educate, Equip, and Empower—the three Es or E3 in everything I do in my lifetime. In addition to being a certified life strategies coach, I serve on a couple of boards centered around helping youth and young adults find their calling and counsel them in career search, career exploration, self-awareness, college searches, and finding scholarships.

Many of these ongoing conversations are about helping someone discover the right path, and finding the steps to reach their goal, objectives, and outcomes. I'm also a youth director at my church. Whether working in higher education or secondary education, I am adamant about diligently working to help Educate, Equip, and Empower the next generation. That is my Purpose!

What Informs My Purpose?

The notion of what informs my Purpose is of profound significance. Looking back at my life, I see different things that have transpired. I think it overlaps with the question of destiny because as I experienced these events, I had to ask, *What am I supposed to get from this? Why did that happen? Why me?* The series of events that happen in your life should lead you to question your destiny. Who am I supposed to be? What or who am I supposed to affect? What impact am I supposed to have in my lifetime? Where am I going?

My Back Story

My parents divorced when I was ten years old, but even when they were married, my dad wasn't around a lot. Of course, I didn't start seeing the emotional and mental impact until my adolescence. I had a lot of anger, resentment, fear, rejection, and abandonment issues. So, I struggled with that for some years. As a result, I didn't have the best relationship with my father. But as I matured, I got into college; and in my young adulthood, I found my faith. Soon, I realized I was not the only one experiencing those kind of events—emotional issues. My father's absence left a gap, a void, that I was constantly trying to fill in different ways.

As I matured and took the time to recenter, regroup, and find myself, I was able to discover there was a need. In the midst of the pain and distress I went through, I found some answers that I could share with other people who have experienced or are experiencing the same type of trials or events that I did—like my dad not being there, the fact that he remarried and had more kids with his new wife, the many times he didn't show up for special events in my life, and the many times he said inappropriate things. During that time, I wasn't aware enough to say, *Wait a minute! That hurts.*

Later, I found out that my dad had the same experiences with his father. Then, after getting to know my grandfather before he passed, I learned that he had also gone through the same thing with his dad. I thought, *Why is this happening? What's happening? Maybe I'm the one that has to bring a stop to this generational problem.* The whole situation with my father and grandfather helped me to understand what it takes to be a father who is present in his children's lives. So, when I had my daughter, I knew I had an idea of what to do and what not to do based on my experiences.

As I got older, my mom always told me life is all about choices. She says there were certain things she saw with her parents growing up that she decided not to repeat with me or my siblings. She would say, "So, it doesn't mean it's easy, but sometimes we go through what is necessary to show what is available to us in life and the choices we have. Juan, you always have a choice. You can decide to be the person that you desire to be, but you have to make that decision for yourself."

Growing up, I often spent a lot of time alone. I was surrounded by many people, a big family, and many siblings. But I still felt alone, like I didn't fit in. When I went to school or to church, wherever I was, it meant something to me to connect with other people. Whenever I saw anyone that looked like they were sad or just going through something that was detrimental, whatever it was, my heart centered on them. I want to connect if people allow me to communicate with them, because I want to provide some joy, whatever that looks like and feels like for them. I want to be a part of that process. This is what I do now.

In my heart, I think, if you are constantly thinking about something, and it frustrates you, perhaps that's the thing that you've been called to speak about to make an impact. For me, I realized it hurts me to see people hurt. So, I need to do what I can to help them.

I came to realize that I was called here. I was put on this Earth to help others by bringing awareness to education or if there are some skill sets people may need to improve, I will help to equip them, to acquire the skills they need so they can be the best version of themselves that they desire to be, or just empower them through our interactions, through our conversations, or just through my life example. That is what my heart is set on. It bothered me to see others go through trials that brought me to my Purpose.

Impacting My Community

In my community, just being a young African American man of color, I am working in partnership with dads. My experience is how society sees and treats fathers, especially fathers of color. I have been taking it upon myself to learn rights, ordinances, and statutes of the different states. So, when we're talking, I can inform the fathers about their rights, telling them they can do this or that and providing them with resources to help them. At any level in my involvement in my community, I'm passionate about being that source of information.

When you figure out who you are, no one can stop you from accomplishing your goals. You are the only person who can get in the way of achieving your goal. When you connect with it, and it drives you, that's the driving force that you have. Nothing can stop you but yourself. Nothing can get in the way; you can choose what you allow to get in front of you and to stop you or slow you down.

That's the contribution I have to my community. Just awareness, be it spirituality, education, or resource, or post-secondary options, whatever that looks like. It is education and awareness. Too often, we are programmed and conditioned to think that this is what we've been dealt with. This is the card, the game, and the hand I must play. If you don't want to play that game, then change the game by having an invitation to the table. Create your table, and then you invite people to it.

My Success Story

My life is going well from the feedback I've received and the connections that I have made and am making. So, there are quite a few individuals that I had met were in middle school, others were in high school, and quite a few of them are still in college and are about to graduate.

I had a young man that I mentored. I have always told him that he is my success story. I met him in his second semester of his freshman year when he was in high school and I was serving as his assistant track coach, and we just connected. He was born and raised in East Tennessee in a lower economic area in what we would call the hood. There was a lot of crime, drugs, and all types of things in his neighborhood that he grew up around.

Now, he lives in Houston, Texas, and is working on his master's degree as a family therapist. We talked about the impact and purpose of everything he went through with his family, the ups and downs, and the estranged relationships, at times, with his mother and father. Currently, he is a relationship coach who's thriving on social media with the connections he's making and putting out content. We meet every other week to check in with updates! It's amazing just watching him.

The level of impact is making a difference, and I see that often. Even the connections I'm making now, even more so with parents. I realized some years ago that it's so easy to say that these kids ended up this way because the parents weren't involved. But I know that sometimes when parents aren't involved, it's not because they don't want to be. Sometimes they can't because of their work schedules or whatever is going on in the family. I have also been working with some parents. I'm finding a way to bring education on all levels. I am considering starting a parent university and bringing in life coaches and mentors who can educate parents on different processes, whether by themselves or just how to move their children along through life, through school, and post-secondary. So that's something that keeps me going. As long as I'm here and if this area is for me, I will give it my all and work diligently to continue to flow with those three Es.

Walking In My Purpose

If you're walking in Purpose, it is where you reside, because if you're walking around, that's where you spend most of your time. So, if you find yourself constantly in a place where you are Walking in Purpose, everything you're doing is tied to why you are here on this Earth, then that's where you live. That is where you find yourself, that's home. So, if that's where your path is laid, your steps should follow the way that leads to your destiny. That's your alignment.

Living intentionally is being aligned with your calling. You could turn the lights off, it could get dark, and I would still know how to move about in my home because I am connected to it. I think about it like this, even when I'm home, seated in this space, I am aware of everything around me because I spend so much time here. I live here; I reside here. I walk around; I walk through here. So, I'm aligned with my living space. It is the same way with Purpose, because I'm here, and I walk in Purpose.

Living in My Purpose

I'm functioning in my Purpose. So even when it gets dark for me, or some things are not going how I want them to, I've been here long enough. I've spent some time in my center and just knowing who I am; I know how to navigate, how to continue to move, put one foot in front of the other, and continue to accomplish and succeed because I'm living on a mission.

You know, a mentor of mine always said, "I don't wake up to light. I don't wake up to a job; I wake up to life." So, what he meant by that is I've worked to find my calling in life. I'm not just going to a job. You shouldn't have to wake me up because I'm excited when I get up. After all, I get to pursue my destiny. What I'm doing is with purpose. So, living with intent is a perspective shift because I think, a lot of times, we may falter just thinking something keeps happening, or if I try that, it's not going to go anywhere. But when I decide I'm going to align my actions with my intentions, I am more in tune with who I am. Since I can choose who I want to be, my movement, choices, involvement, interactions, whatever it is, will be more meaningful because I want to live on Purpose.

Importance of Mentorship

When I look back at some of my successes and failures in life as a young adult, about twenty-five or twenty-six years old, I'm thankful that I had certain individuals in my life that took it upon themselves to say, "Hey, don't go that way, or hey, have you tried this? Did you realize that you seem to be this type of person? You seem to enjoy this, you know, maybe give some thought to that." I had people helping to guide me along my way by coaching and advising me regarding business, spirituality, family, education, and all those different things in life. And they helped me discover that passion to identify myself and help me figure out how to navigate certain things going on in life. I realized that I am a product of mentorship. I didn't get here on my own.

I remember entering my master's program in college. At the time, Robert Kiyosaki's book, *Rich Dad Poor Dad*, was blowing up. We started reading it at my church. Kiyosaki talked about how it wasn't a diss to his biological father, but the principles his biological father taught him didn't help him strive or accomplish much in life. But he had a mentor who taught him different things about finances and stuff like that.

At the time I read that book, for me, the two characters represented Dr. Stephenson and my biological father. Although there were things I learned from my biological dad, my rich Dad was Dr. Stephenson, because when he was teaching and talking to me about real estate, the market, and improving myself, regardless of where I had come from, he helped me to see that I could better myself so I could impact the community and my family. Not only did he talk to me about it, but he also taught his daughters, Tremaine and Kiana, their friends, nieces, nephews, and siblings. Those were lessons that I had to discover from my connection with my actual father. I saw Dr. Stephenson living that example. So he played that role of my rich Dad for a long time.

It all started when I met Kiana when we were fifteen or sixteen years old. I started coming over to Dr. Stephenson's house just sitting around him and learning. I was thinking, *How does he know so much? He's so driven.* He always took the time to throw little nuggets of wisdom out there, challenging stuff. That's where it started with the mentorship, not realizing it was mentorship at that time. I realized that the words he was leaving with me were impactful. But I have never had the opportunity or taken the opportunity to tell him before now how much he's impacted my life as my mentor.

My Inner Circle

As far back as I can remember, the conversation about Purpose has been ongoing, and the word purpose may not have been used every time in the discussion, but it's always been a question of Why are you here? Why do you exist? What are you going to be in life? What are you going to do? What level of impact do you want to have in your lifetime?

As I start to figure my life out, I have had a close friend say he watched me face challenges, and the way I came through inspired him. Conversations like that start to help someone, and that feels good. And now that person is walking in their Purpose or doing what they had always prayed or desired to do. So, there is something to this.

In my family and circle of friends, the reason for our existence was always central to our relationships and friendships. Whenever I was around, the recurring theme I constantly heard was about my destiny. For instance, when I discuss something with a mentor, family member, or friend, I might mention, "Hey, this fits right into your narrative or aligns with your principles." They'd invariably respond, "Yes, it aligns with my purpose." And I would think, "Indeed, it does."

Finding Purpose

Regardless of where we find ourselves, it gets better because there is a reason why we exist. In finding that, take the time to ask those fundamental questions. And it doesn't start with asking folks around you the question—ask yourself those questions. What do I care about the most? What catches my attention? What is something I can't stop thinking about when I wake up? What is the first thing on my mind when I see that brink of light that breaks my heart? Ask those questions because I promise you, what you are called to do is discovered in gaining the answers to those questions, you find yourself in some level of awareness, self-awareness, while finding solutions to those questions.

I would engage myself. And you should engage yourself—that means setting aside time or finding that quiet moment when you just cut everything off. Sometimes I'll tell people it's not necessarily that you have to quit externalities. Sometimes, it's even what's going on the inside. So, in finding those quiet moments, you can better engage yourself. But it takes intentionality; it doesn't just happen. And sometimes, moments happen a lot that we miss because we're just not in sync. The more intentional we become, we begin to understand and have that introspection where we can trust our vision and life that our outlook and even our self-reflection begin to make more sense.

My Legacy

When it is all said and done, I want people to say that I am better because he existed. His life mattered. If this could be said, I want them to know. I want them to say it matters that he exists.

Who Checked Me?

I believe in God, and many of my conversations are with him. Sometimes, a moral compass directs me, saying, *No, too far left.* I value my walk, my belief in God, and the conversations with him. At times, he speaks to me or sends individuals to help guide me. For example, my mom is a voice in my life, a strong voice. Now, fortunately, my father is also. As we both got older, our lives have changed for the better. We talk more than we did when I was growing up. My dad is a voice of wisdom in my ear telling me I can be better. My response is, "I want and need to do this, but it's not over! It's not over just because it didn't go how we wanted it to."

Mahatma Gandhi said, "If we could change ourselves, the tendencies in the world would also change." And even when others are still trying to discover what their life is about, ask yourself, What am I going to do? Start there, be the change that you want to see. What is it that you want to see differently? What is something that catches your attention?

What do you wish for? For example, when you look at something and think, if this was just different, if they created that, if they built this, or if they had that, whatever that is, be the change, or if you see something that shouldn't be that way and it frustrates you, be the change that you want to see."

Dr. Stephenson once told me, "It is in pursuit that will lead you to your true calling. You will find yourself walking in your Purpose, living on Purpose, and aligned with your Purpose."

Puzzled, I asked, "Is it okay if it doesn't make sense right now?"

"Don't stop. Keep going because it will," he said.

Throughout my life, I've thought about this, but Dr. Stephenson helped me to understand it more clearly. He provided his wisdom, and it stretched my point of view. I am forever grateful for my connection to him and fully understand that a conversation about our life's journey is critical in our community and the world. The world would be better off if we all took the time to pursue our Purpose and understand it.

I use the following story with a lot of my mentees. I grew up with Marvel and DC Comics. So, I remember when Superman II came out in 1980, this movie was focused on Superman's struggle with understanding why he was put on earth. Now, mind you, he is different from everybody else, but because of his Purpose and what he was called to Earth to do, he wasn't allowed to live his life like everybody else. So, he couldn't be with the person he fell in love with, because he realized that it could cost her life if he stayed with her.

So, Superman got frustrated because he couldn't live life like everyone else. So, he decided he was not going to be Superman. He was just going to be Clark Kent. He gave up. And throughout the whole movie, you see him wrestling with his emotions. He saw people getting killed, and robbed, and crime kept growing. And he thought, *I was called to do something about this, but I don't want to do it because I want to live my life. I want to be like everybody else. I want to live. I want to love who I love.* But he finally realized that's what he was here to do. Purpose sometimes comes with sacrifice. So, he eventually accepted his responsibility, and put the cape back on and went back to work.

Remember, you're called, and it is a commitment. You should respond with, "I am willing, and I'm able. I'm going to do the work, and I can't keep running. I'm ready."

Homelessness

"With homelessness, you don't necessarily
have to be under a bridge somewhere."

Diana Clarke

Diana Clarke is a humbled servant and a woman of grace. She is a registered nurse in the state of Georgia and holds a master's degree in theology and a doctorate in ministry. Miss Clarke is the founder and CEO of Diamond's Well Place, a 501c3 non-profit organization in Cobb County, Georgia, that helps single mothers who are experiencing homelessness.

My Early Years

I was born in Jamaica, West Indies, and I grew up in the parish of St Andrew. I spent my formative years in the Cypress Hall district and Stony Hill. I attended Meadowbrook High School and graduated at the age of fifteen. I later attended the West Avenue Institute and Excelsior Community College. Most of what I remember about my early days in Jamaica is that my family was impoverished, but we were happy. We didn't have the best clothes and nutritious food, but we had faith. I always dreamt of becoming better in life and escaping poverty. My father was mainly in the United States for most of my childhood; my mother and grandmother raised me. I migrated to the United States at seventeen with my two brothers, Omar and Dowayne. Understanding the importance of education, I didn't hesitate to enroll in college when I could.

Purpose Defined

Purpose is my reason for existing. It is why I am on this earth and, ultimately, what I'm supposed to fulfill when I go through the journey.

Importance of Purpose

If you do not have an understanding of your Purpose, you won't have a fulfilled life. You will be thrown back and forth like the wind, having no regard for what you do daily and no understanding of why you are here as a human being.

My Purpose

My Purpose is not easily defined because I am the only one who can truly understand it fully. When I look back at my life, the things I have walked through, and where I am now, I can see the path where I'm supposed to be going, and I am at peace with that path. I can say that my Purpose is influencing others.

I consider myself to be a survivor because I have survived many things in life in terms of traumas—different things that I have been through.

I have gone through an educational path I started off not grasping but grew to understand. There are so many other people out there who might not fully comprehend their path, so they're looking for answers. I do believe I have a lot of answers for them.

I am a humble servant and a woman of grace. I am strong in terms of my faith in something outside of myself that is directing me, and I submit to that. Faith is defined by my foundational beliefs, the substance of things hoped for, the evidence of things not seen. Faith to me is being able to manifest my strongest desires. And I serve a cause for the betterment of humanity, the betterment of women. I serve a cause that goes beyond what I see in the natural. That's why I am saying that my purpose will not be easily understood by others. But I will try my best to articulate it.

The Work I Am Called to Do

I have walked through a path where I was in a position of homelessness. With homelessness, you don't necessarily have to be under a bridge somewhere. There are tons of people who might not have a roof over their heads. They may be staying with someone, but the place is not theirs, and they just have this feeling of displacement, a lack of belonging. You could even be in a situation where you're staying with your mother or father, but you don't find your place there. You don't have a place of belonging. You don't own it; it's not yours. While you are going through this transitional period, you just need to feel a sense of being connected to someone or something like, you own this. This is where you need to be. I've been through that process. I have walked through it. I understand it.

Now, because of my past and what I've been through, I am operating Diamonds Wealth Place, a nonprofit organization that helps single mothers who are experiencing homelessness. I call it a ministry. We are building this organization out of a place of understanding and related ability. I can operate this ministry and know that I am walking in my Purpose.

Walking in My Purpose

I didn't just come to the earth to eat, breathe, sleep, wake up, make some money, and have fun. That was not the only Purpose. Yes, it is important to do these things. It is important to live life to the fullest. At the same time, are you helping someone else along the way? Are you able to pull someone else up so that they can enjoy the benefits this earth has? When I talk about walking in my Purpose, I think, *How much am I giving back to my community? How much am I doing that makes me feel fulfilled as a human being?* Not everybody may feel the same way. Some people may have the mindset of, *Let me just love me. Let me just take care of myself.* But to some people, that is not fulfilling to just take care of themselves.

How Do I Know When I Am Walking In My Purpose?

I know I am walking in my Purpose! Something extraordinary happens when you are walking in your Purpose. It is that gut feeling and confidence that I am doing the right thing, and there is peace about it. I am not here just willy-nilly getting up and doing something because I feel like this right now. No, there is this deep inner belief, this deep inner conviction that I am doing the right thing, that this is what makes me feel fulfilled as a human being. And it is not like you are out here trying to make a name for yourself. That is another important thing to consider because from my foundation, and what influences me, it is like God saying, "I will make your name great (2 Samuel 7 NIV)." And it is not like you're all here trying to make a name for yourselves. You're out here just trying to make sure that you are doing things that are following your moral compass. At the same time, you have peace about it.

How To Find Purpose

Too many people do not have a sense of their Purpose. One of the things that I would tell them is not to try to take on a task that they are not prepared for. Do not do anything when you are anxious. Just try to listen to that inner being, that thing within you that brings you peace, because you may be going through a lot of things and thinking, *I want to do this, or I want to do that.* But you must wait until you are in a place of stillness. That is when you really want to dig deep and

ask yourself, *Is this what I'm supposed to be doing? Am I feeling fulfilled when I do it?* You want to be at peace with it. Because whenever you're doing something when you're anxious, it will never be the right thing to do. Intentionality and mental clarity are extremely important to help you feel at peace.

My Collision With My Purpose

The discovery of my Purpose came about because of a series of events. In 1998, when I was pregnant with my first child, I was homeless. That is when I had my collision with my Purpose because my eyes opened to a world outside of what I was living in, and I didn't know it existed. Based on the help I received, I was like, *Oh, this is what I'm supposed to be doing when I'm stronger and restored.* This is what I'm supposed to be doing now, from 1998 until 2022 is a long time, a very long time. It took me through a series of experiences, not just my circumstances, but other people's circumstances—counseling other women who were going through similar situations, not just women from my walk of life, but women from all walks of life. I realized that it was a problem, one that I had committed my mind to work through, but I had not done anything about it. However, it came time for me to move forward in what I had promised myself to do back in 1998.

What Informs My Purpose

I have done studies in theology and have a doctorate in ministry. Prior to studying theology and ministry, I had been educated in business. I graduated from Baruch College with a business administration degree. I was very young and was adamant about doing that, even though I knew I was being called to a higher level. But I wanted to be a businesswoman, and that's it. So, I went and got my master's degree in business administration. However, there was still a tug on my heart that I was out of alignment with what I was supposed to be doing. I worked in the mortgage industry for two years until 2014, when I had to fly to New York to visit this young lady. She was a single mom living on the streets in Queens, New York. I had to fly there with someone else to get her off the street. Then, we took her to Kings County Hospital, where she received mental health treatment.

It was there that my eyes opened again to my Purpose. And I thought, *Diana, you're not doing what you're supposed to be doing.* As a result, I began studying again because I was out of alignment and because of that tug on my heart—that deep inner conviction when you are not doing what you're supposed to be doing, yet you know this is your area of influence, and it is what you were created to do.

You can work in a business industry all you want, but at the same time you will not be fulfilled. I truly enjoyed helping that young lady. And that's when I knew I needed to go back and study again. I was also working in the church. During that time, I was married to a pastor, and I saw all the different facets of people's lives. If I went back to school to study ministry on a different level, I could affect the lives of people. So that's why I returned to school because it was just bad out there in terms of lack of the Word and lack of understanding. I thought, *Who can God trust to study this thing and impart it to people so that it influences their lives and causes some type of change?* And I said, *Okay, it's me.* That is why I went back to Bible school and studied. I decided that I was going to go all the way through. You can't go any further than getting a doctorate.

Going to Kings County Hospital is where the light bulb went off for me. My mind was opened to another level of enlightenment. What I experienced in the mental health unit was that the patients were primarily women, mainly African American, but many were from the Caribbean. I thought to myself, *This is really, truly an epidemic.* My mom worked in the mental health unit then, and she would tell me different stories she encountered there. I thought to myself, my studies need to be geared towards doing something about this population—women who were disenfranchised, women coming out of certain types of relationships, having children, and just being dragged down with the burdens of life. I needed to walk in that path. This did not happen overnight. I was struggling, wrestling with myself and saying, *This is not going to make you any money. You're not going to get rich doing this. You're not going to get anywhere doing this in terms of the things of the world.* But it was a cause that called me, and I knew it.

My Newfound Maturity and Riches

When you're younger, you think a certain way until you begin to experience things in life, then your mindset begins to change. So back then, my definition of riches was stuff, material things. Now I define riches as my mental health, peace, joy, tranquility, and lack of stress. When you are at a place where you're walking in your Purpose, your whole sense of being, your understanding of life is just on a different level, and it feels good, like a heavenly feeling. You know you are at peace with yourself and genuinely confident about who you are and what you're here to do. There's no better definition than it feels like heaven. You have transcended to the place of peace.

The Discussion About Purpose in My Circle of Friends

Well, my circle of friends is small. The world turned upside down with the Covid pandemic and the world economy did, too. Now, everybody is aware that anything can change at any minute. So, we're all relooking at what we are here for.

I am doing what I'm supposed to be doing, but am I fulfilled? I noticed this has become a trend. People want to live fulfilled lives. They don't want to be out here living aimlessly. Some say we are still experimenting. Some people repurposed their lives and began to look at things differently. Because of that, you are seeing a different level of discussion in your circle of friends. People are even shifting their spirituality. their religions. Some who used to be Christians, are not Christians anymore. Some of them are new age, and some of them have gone into spirituality only. People are searching for their Purpose.

My Thoughts About the Younger Generation

I don't want to speak broadly or just from my experience, but I believe the younger generation has become numb to certain things. They are living aimlessly, and we may need to forgive them. I have young children, and they're just going about living. However, as a parent, you try to instill specific values in them, but again, they will have to live their own lives and have their own experiences. Along the way, your children will be enlightened. That's how I look at it. Some may be a messiah or someone special one day. But generally, they are not seeking their Purpose.

As parents, we want to watch our children and watch their gifting. I have three daughters. I tell them that I know exactly who they are because it was shown to me. I notice tendencies and proclivities, and I might say this child will be functioning in that role, and my other daughter might be take on something different. I can guide them towards a path, but they are still going to have to make their own decisions. But at least I'm giving them the foundation to believe in themselves, trust their heart, and try to ensure they are serving something greater than themselves. These are things that I instill in my girls. They are loving girls, and I am so grateful for my children. I would encourage any parent not to force their kid to become who they want them to be, but try to figure out who they are, and then try to encourage them to be who they are supposed to be.

My Advice About How to Find Purpose

For those individuals who are having difficulties finding their Purpose and are not connecting with their sense of being, they need to spend some time in solitude and search within their souls to find out exactly who they are. Is it easily done? Not necessarily, but you have to find your Purpose for yourself. It cannot be just because someone told you what it is. It will be a series of events that happened throughout your life. Look back to when you were a child and follow the patterns— this happened to me when I was a child, or that happened to me, but I survived this. Look back at your experiences from when you were coming up, and that will probably help you. I am saying probably because this is what helped me, and I am just sharing it with you. However, you cannot just listen to someone else preaching from a pulpit telling you this is what your Purpose is. And you cannot just listen to videos or someone telling you that is what you are destined to do. You will find your calling within you, so be introspective and engage in self-reflection.

Takeaway

For the time that we are living on earth, everybody must find out their Purpose because you're going to have something that I need, and I may have something you need. Each one helps the other because I can't do it all alone. I am going to say this, we are ascending to a higher level of understanding now. Everybody must spend time with themselves, find out who they are, and how they will impact someone else. And let's walk this out together because I don't have it all. I am called to help women, and we are all here to help one another through the journey.

Embarrassed By Who I Was

"You can't help someone who's not willing to participate in their own rescue."

Nafis Ahmed

Nafis Ahmed was born and raised in New York, navigating life and embracing the journey of adulthood. He wears many hats as an entrepreneur, but his most important role is being a "self-improvement junkie." Nafis' ultimate goal is to succeed so he can help those around him and give his mom the life she deserves. His Mantra: "You don't have to be great to start; you have to start to be great."

My Early Years

I was born the same year my mom migrated to the United States. She has done so much for me without help from anyone because we never had anyone except ourselves. So, for me to go about my life the way I was going was an insult to the immense amount of work she had put in to give me life. She is one of the most beautiful women I've known. I'm not saying this because she's my mother. She truly is, and that is why I live by a certain code in life where my morals and integrity are one. I will not compromise for anyone, not even myself, because at the end of the day, even if I can't attain the success I'm striving for, at least I know that I'm a good person and that is enough to put a smile on my mom's face. My mom didn't have the word "no" in her vocabulary because she always tried her best to give me everything I wanted as a child. Now, even though I'm twenty-six years old, she would give up her life for me, if needed, and I can say that wholeheartedly. She does not have a single selfish bone in her body regarding me.

What is Purpose?

Purpose is something people want to be known for. It can be like an end goal for people where they try to let that be the definition of who they are. People can find their identity of who they're meant to be or want to be by pursuing their purpose through the trials and tribulations life has to offer. You either strive to be that, or you don't, and most people, including me, tend to live their life on autopilot for a very long time. We may be very emotional beings. From my experience, my emotions would dictate my actions, indicating that I never really had any control over my life or future.

My Purpose Defined

My purpose is to create a better life for myself, but more so for my mom. My mom is a key inspiration in my drive to become a better version of myself. Success is inevitable and bound to happen because I believe in my purpose. I can accomplish anything I want if I keep pursuing my dreams. Regardless of how stagnant life may seem, I can achieve my goals by becoming a better me every day. Still, I know my 100 percent today is better than yesterday's 100 percent. I rely on discipline and live by a certain code, whereas I truly believe the law of attraction is real. I gravitate towards like-minded people, or those individuals will gravitate towards me, because success doesn't have to be a lonely road, and you can always find beautiful souls that align with what you seek out of life, making your purpose much more meaningful.

I want to give back everything life offers because no one else will provide that to us except ourselves. So, that has become my drive and purpose in life. My aim for success includes being financially free and becoming a better human being, but more so, being a better person than just from the financial aspect. When you're rich, life will still be hard because so many issues may come with money, and that's due to everyone chasing after the high that money brings. They forget to look within themselves, which is where emotional intelligence comes into play because if you want to be good to another individual in life, you have to be good to yourself first, or you're just pouring oil on a fire that'll only keep burning till you run out of oil to keep the flame on. One day, the rain washes away all the hard work you've put in to create something you never really focused on, which is the foundation to keep the flame burning regardless of the storm.

My Collision with Purpose

I had a collision with my purpose two and a half years ago. It was eye-opening. During this time, I took myself off autopilot for the first time. Covid lockdown showed me I needed to make a change in my life.

Things had gotten to a point where I did not think about my future, nor had I spent the amount of alone time with myself as I did during the first couple of months of lockdown. I was so busy living on a cycle that kept repeating itself. As I got older, I asked what I was truly doing with my life. I needed to break out of that cycle because I didn't want to be this person when I got older, especially since my mom had been taking care of me most of my life, and she was a single parent. So, for her sake, I needed to come to terms with a life that had already happened. There's nothing that can be done about the past. I now realize that all I can do is curate my future in the present because time isn't something we can ever control; every minute is a memory that will never be gained back. I grew up with so many memories not worth remembering and nothing to reflect on that can bring me joy. Now that I am on a new journey, I'm starting to appreciate life for what it is.

In the last two and a half years, I've become a mental health advocate, because I initially didn't know I had a severe case of attention-deficit/hyperactivity disorder (ADHD), which has affected me immensely throughout my entire life where I truly felt like my life was always empty and that I would never amount to anything in life due to that belief. I felt so little of myself, and I was always in a depressed state of mind where I used to indulge on things that would bring me temporary pleasure or happiness in life by putting a band-aid on my wound rather than dealing with the issue that just kept bleeding when the bandage kept wearing off. That was when I found out about my diagnosis. I got on track with medicine to regulate my dopamine levels within the last two and a half years. I have completely changed. Anyone that knew me then and knows me now can attest to the fact that I worked so hard to get to where I currently am. However, most people that knew me before don't know me now. It was just one chapter in my life with many different chapters ahead leading to a different and better version of myself.

I am much more in my skin rather than letting thoughts linger about what others may think of me. I used to put up a wall because I felt embarrassed about who I was. The people in my family were so successful in life. At the same time, I had nothing going for me, which was used as an excuse to dig myself deeper in a hole, making it harder for me to get out. Still, I have no regrets about doing so, because I wouldn't be who I am today if I hadn't gone through what life has presented to me thus far. I can change most things about my life because it is in my hands to determine what I want out of life.

There was a friend of mine that I used to consider very dear to me, Coumba. He was a year younger than I was. When Covid lockdown happened, he prioritized building a better life for himself rather than doing what I was doing, dwelling on the past. He had plans to build a club. I saw him bring his vision of what I had in mind, come to fruition. Seeing the hard work he put in as an immigrant to this country for about ten years and accomplish what he has done was truly inspiring to me and forced me to think about life in the same ideology.

You can't just pray for life to give you what you want; you must work for it. The people you choose to be around can play a significant role in your life. If you want to attract good people in your life, you must be a good person first. As much as people want to negate this idea, energy is contagious. I know that to be true because I've started to put myself at tables that I never thought I'd get a chance to sit at, but I had to separate myself from people who had different values in life in order to have a seat at these tables.

What Values and Beliefs Drives Me in Pursuit of My Purpose

My mom has been divorced for a long time. I never had a father figure; my mom was my mother and father in one. I needed to become a better individual in all aspects of life to give back a percentage of what she has done for me. Being a good person was my backup plan, even if only financially. I could give her the life she deserved. I knew she'd be happy knowing I'd be the man she wanted her son to be. So I took it into account being both financially free, where we have the money to buy anything life offers, and just being a good soul.

This has afforded me to attract beautiful souls in my life, Raisa is one of them. She has stuck with me and believed in me at times when life has been so stressful— trying to change my life where I started to lose belief in myself or thinking that I wouldn't be able to get to where I am now. Those beautiful souls can help create the time that passes by a beautiful memory to look back on.

I have become a successful entrepreneur, and I realize as I keep growing, I'm transforming into a better version of myself. The person you used to be will always be the person you fear the most. Here are a few quotes that I picked up along my journey that motivated me and may encourage you: "You don't have to be great to start; you must start to be great." And, "You can't wait until life isn't hard anymore before you decide to be happy. You can change who you want to be with a snap of your finger. It's up to you how hungry you are and how badly you want it."

Having Discipline

If anyone ever asks me how I got to where I am now, I will tell them that discipline is the main factor in attaining what I want. One percent every day can add up to 100 percent after 100 days. It does not matter if you don't notice any progress when you're at 5–10 percent. However, once you know you've gotten to 50 percent, from my own experience, I know that I will not stop doing what I do because after I experienced feeling stagnant in the early stages, now I know that I'm growing. I've become aware that I genuinely enjoy learning what life offers, and I'm learning more about myself as I take each step. We're all human. We all grow up with habits we've become accustomed to and think about. *That it's just who we are*, but most times, that isn't the case. We all have flaws and bad habits from childhood into adulthood. Unwinding those bad habits is something most people need to do; it's crucial. I know because I used to be one of them. I was in airplane mode. I never did anything with intention. I wanted to go wherever life took me.

We are often afraid of the unknown, which is uncomfortable, because we put ourselves in a comfortable place of dealing with the unpleasantry of life and breaking out of that is scary. I completely understand, but to change and get from where we are now to where we want to be, we must look in the mirror and understand why we were who we were and how we changed that to improve.

Once you start putting yourself in the process of facing yourself, I guarantee that most people would be grateful that they've done so. It's an excellent way to reflect on the person you used to be but aren't anymore, especially when you know you've outgrown that previous version of you who once didn't know any better. There is more to life than the box that we've chosen to be stuck in.

I realize that I can manifest whatever I put my mind to. I can become a doctor, a lawyer, etc. And this is coming from someone who lived with ADHD. School was tough for me, so much so that I did not graduate from high school. Due to the way I was, I was not supposed to graduate from elementary or middle school. Once I put myself together and achieved what I have accomplished, I know if I can do it, so can anyone else if they want to.

Fear of What's on The Other Side of Reality

Yes, it was a fear that I wouldn't be able to give my mom the life that she deserves, and she's getting older. I wasn't doing anything to make it happen. She's done so much for me; the least I can do is to be a better person and give her the life she deserves because no one else would do it for her, and no one else would do what she has done for me.

I have gone through a lot of ordeals in the process of trying to be a better person, and I know I'll keep coming across those problems. As long as I keep swinging past them, I will be better at handling them every single time, regardless of what life throws at me. Also, I just want to show love to the people I care about by being able to give them what they deserve in life, aside from my mom. At my lowest points in life, there were very few people who had been there for me. That in itself is something I will always cherish about them. I want to be able to give back in ways unimaginable because I know they didn't have to do what they did for me. I want to show them that I care about them and if I can help them, I will. I don't need any gratitude or anything for it. Knowing that I could do something for them is good enough for me. I've discovered that when you see a smooth future, speed bumps today do not matter.

Living my Purpose

As with everything in life, pursuing your purpose is a process. There are so many obstacles that I have come across that I've never dealt with before, nor did I expect them to come up the way they did. Whenever those obstacles arose, I felt like I took those hits pretty hard. But every single time I kept figuring out how to get over them, I felt like a new, improved version of myself because it forced me to take a step back and look at the entire situation as to why this took place and how I was going to bulldoze over those situations that I've come across. Over the last two years, as I kept doing this over and over again, I've gotten more confident in myself in knowing that I can take on anything that comes my way that may have crippled the old me. Knowing this about me has been very fulfilling because I stopped worrying about problems when they took place; I just started prioritizing myself on figuring out a solution to the problem. This has made my purpose meaningful because life can kick anyone's ass anytime. It's all about how you take that kick and keep moving forward because as you take those hits, you get better at handling them and picking up experience to know what to do and what not to do next time in life to have a better life.

My Advice

I am sure plenty of people have taken wrong turns in life that led to a path that felt like they had wasted their life and that there was nothing they could do to change it. However, I'm a testimony to the fact that it is never too late to change your life. It is always possible to learn, regardless of what you know. There is no reason to keep ourselves stuck in a box when there's so much to live for and learn from different cultures and different perspectives. Why not try different experiences to give your life more meaning?

My advice is to learn from everyone but do not follow anyone. Be your own person, stand on what you truly believe, and only readjust if it's for the betterment of yourself and the people around you. Grow with people that want to attain more out of life, but make sure those people are good people, and that they want the same thing as you. Make sure you avoid distractions. They may seem appealing, but those distractions will separate you from your goals and the life that you truly want.

My Outlook

I genuinely enjoy being productive, and I'm a happy self-improvement junkie, because if I don't feel like I did anything that made me better today, I don't feel so well with myself. That's why it's become like a drug for me, in the sense that it gives me the fulfillment I need to keep myself pushing. There isn't any limit to anything in life, and we can truly get whatever we want if we work towards it and manifest it. Be cautious about the people you choose to be around because people may look very appealing to the eyes; however, be aware of the words they speak and their actions. Be very careful as you honestly assess yourself and make the same assessment about the people you choose to associate with because energy is contagious, whether it's good or bad energy. Keep in mind that art imitates life, and life imitates art. Be your own artist, draw what you want from life, and turn it into existence.

Who Checked Me?

Raisa and my mom are the only individuals in my life that I truly care about. If it weren't for these two, I would not have been able to face those obstacles that life has thrown at me lately. Their belief in me was enough for me to keep pushing and to figure out everything that came my way with a solution to make my life better and not have that same obstacle ever make me feel handicapped. I'm truly grateful for Raisa because individuals like her are hard to come across. I love this girl for being there for me even when I didn't feel like being there for myself.

Lessons I Share

The takeaway is to be truly a good person and good to others. You must prioritize yourself above anyone else because you can't be good to anyone if you're not good to yourself. Just know that life isn't just about repeating one chapter throughout the book; we can recreate the book anytime that we want. It's just a matter of how badly we want something, and if we want it badly enough, the chapter will start writing itself as we pursue attaining it, which can be used as a purpose in your life. My purpose is to provide for the people I care about and live a fruitful life through the hard work I know I'm putting in.

My Challenge

One of the primary challenges I've faced in pursuing my purpose is having ADHD. I felt hopeless throughout my entire life because ADHD severely handicapped me. I felt like I would not amount to anything in life.

How I Want to Be Remembered

I want to be remembered as someone who aimed for a better life and got it. I turned "nothing" into "something."

Last Word

Value people who stand on what they believe. I value people for what they bring to the table. What value do you bring to my life, and what kind of value can I bring to your life to make you a better person and vice versa? You can learn a thing or two from everybody in life, but you must be open to learning. Refrain from changing who you are unless the change adds value and gives you a better perspective on life. Trust people for who they are, but make sure you trust yourself first and know that you'll be ok regardless of whatever they do, even if they do right or wrong by you. Life doesn't have to be as complicated as we make it out to be; but understand that there will always be a way out. We must keep searching for it. The critical driver in my inspiration to find and fulfill my purpose is my mom. I wholeheartedly love you, Ammu, and will do everything for you.

From Rural Farmer To High School Principal

"Purpose that is well served is a purpose that positively impacts others."

Garfield James

Garfield James is a husband, a father, and the principal of Little London High School in Westmoreland, Jamaica. He is the sitting Councillor for Sheffield Division, a member of Parliament aspirant for Western Westmoreland, a business owner, and a registered farmer specializing in forestry. He is a real estate developer and an advocate for positive social change.

My Early Years

I am fortunate to have grown up with my parents, who are a very integral part of my childhood development. I grew up in a large extended family with twelve individuals, and we were a close-knit family. For me, this was a very normal situation. The nurturing I got was second to none.

We had the opportunity to socialize, share, and build excellent interpersonal relationships.

However, there were more mouths to feed than what was available to eat. Scarce resources led to challenging situations but provided an experience and opportunity to learn and develop some very important life lessons. I learned how to manage and address challenges, to work with limited resources, and to be my brother's keeper. I have no regrets. I look back and am thankful for that opportunity.

Am I Experiencing My Purpose?

I started farming at the tender age of eleven while growing up in Clarendon, a parish in Jamaica. I did this to earn additional income to assist with family expenditures. This need pushed me to extend farming to where I could now supply vendors in and around my community. I was engaged in that process for approximately ten years before I moved on to include forestry. That experience helped me to recognize and create my purpose.

What Is My Purpose?

Purpose is why we exist. The actual expression and the engagement one shares will define one's reason for being born. Therefore, a person's sense of resolution and determination straightforwardly leads to why he is on earth. We are created to serve specific roles in our lifetime. Once you engage in any activity, that action defines why you are made. One may ask if an action ends up being negative, does that action represent one's purpose, or does it only constitute positive actions? Whatever one does, it is evident that the reason for their existence can be positive or negative. However, one must seek to be involved in practices that result in positive outcomes.

Importance of Purpose

The consequences for understanding your existence can be very significant in that it can impact not only an individual, a group, or an organization, but an entire nation. You are not only fulfilling your God-given duty, but you are enabling others to share their understanding of and pursue their destiny.

If it is God's will for me to plant trees so that sometime later, I can obtain money by selling them to you; however, if I forget to plant the trees, at some point, the access to that resource might be limited. I would have failed to carry out my God-given duty and responsibility to live in my purpose and end up affecting someone else. If we fail to implement actions and duties that we are called to do, then it could affect somebody in a very negative way.

Being an experienced educator enables me to carry out my role and responsibility efficiently and effectively. I can educate and provide opportunities for any audience and will continue to do so. Every aspect of life, everything we do, carries a concept and the meaning of why we exist. We will all do something in a way that determines and highlights the benefits of understanding the reason for our existence.

I Have a Simple Purpose

My purpose is simple but has many branches. I provide enormous support daily. I am a husband, and a father which means I have many responsibilities and roles to fulfil. I am an educator. I interface with hundreds of students, as well as their parents and stakeholders of the institution I manage. I provide services in the form of counseling, giving advice and a listening ear when necessary.

I am a Justice of Peace. It is a critical function that engages and works with community members in providing services such as dealing with documents, arrests, bonds, and other areas of verification. As a businessman, many individuals rely on my ability to carry out my purpose in that area. Should I fail to manage effectively, it may result in someone not being able to adequately put food on the table, or to pay their bills. I am a farmer. People rely heavily on the fact that I can support the food industry and the building industry. I produce materials used to build furniture and for construction. If I fail to fulfill that objective, someone might not be able to find the resources needed to fulfill their calling for their family and even for society.

So, it is my responsibility to live my purpose. It's an enormous service. And periodically there are frustrations, depending on which task is attended to on any given day. But I am learning to be able to live through motivation and self-actualization.

There are times when you will face challenges in life. For example, there are times I feel like I want to remove a specific task for which I was given an enormous responsibility to implement and fulfill. However, when I look at how others would be affected, I realize that I would be removing reality from those that rely on me, and that is not my purpose.

The very act of following your destined path can sometimes lead to stress and depression but most often there is an extrinsic motivation to continue. So, although your calling sometimes brings sadness and stress, the joy it brings is more rewarding. In a bad situation, one's life's work may occasionally lead to depression. That is when the big questions are asked: Am I living intentionally? Should I change my life's direction? Where can I get the right advice? How do I manage or deal with that? These questions may be answered internally or by external assistance.

It is important to note that while serving and living your purpose, there may be challenges, pressure, and stress. However, one must never seek to give up on living one's purpose but find ways to overcome obstacles and achieve the objective of living your purpose.

Transitioning To Become an Educator, A Teacher

I grew up predominantly in a rural community. Many youngsters then were looking towards farming activities, especially vegetables, and sugarcane. I was heavily engaged in youth programs through the church of God in Jamaica. From these experiences, I recognized that many youngsters in my age group, teenagers, didn't understand their purpose. They did not have big dreams like me. They didn't see me as someone aspiring to greater heights. So, I used this opportunity to demonstrate to them that despite being in that small rural community, dominated by peasant farming, they could dream big and achieve anything they wanted.

I started fulfilling my dreams by getting the required certification so I could come back to the local school in my community and help them. I spent a few years there, worked with some youth programs, brought in some additional support from external agencies, and created some important experiences for youngsters. Many of them utilized these programs, did very well, and became successful men and women, not only in Jamaica but globally. Thus, I became a teacher as well as a role model.

One of my greatest achievements is to see that from an early age, through my intervention, many people were not just dreaming big, but were now thinking outside the box. Having motivated and influenced them as well as providing opportunities, I became their role model. My purpose had reached the point where I could directly and indirectly assist others, which provided a platform where extrinsic values could be used as a driving force to do well. I am grateful for that opportunity.

My dream was to concentrate on farming as my main way to survive until someone recognized my purpose. That person was Mrs. Winifred MacDonald, an educator, who saw the potential in me and impressed upon me to dream big with an attitude of "The sky is the limit!" If she had not fulfilled her calling or carried out the required actions to help me, I would not be here today sharing my story with "A Collision with Purpose Project." So, it is crucial for us to be fearless in our efforts to pursue why we were created. Because if we don't, we may rob somebody of the opportunity to fulfill their destiny.

From An Eleven-Year-Old Farmer to High School Principal

It is wonderful that many students can share my story, coming from humble beginnings and wanting to dream big, and to achieve much. It provides me with an excellent opportunity to guide the process of facilitating them in achieving their highest potential in terms of education.

It is a great opportunity to lead an institution where you get the chance to board that ship in the lives of youngsters. You also get the opportunity to motivate, guide, share and work with professionals as they fulfill their purpose. It's a tremendous responsibility, but I am grateful for the opportunity, and I will continue to impact lives in a positive way.

Currently, my school, Little London High School, has a student population of 876 students. The number varies depending on migration and environmental changes. Fifty-six teachers are on staff. I have an administrative support staff of forty members and an ancillary staff of twelve. It is a tremendous responsibility, but with an awesome group of individuals working together, we can achieve the administration's objectives.

I have been a principal since 2012. My achievements are many, but I want to highlight the critical aspects of the school in terms of the culture. The culture that existed before 2012 was one of hostility. High conflicts led to physical damage and many expulsions, police involvement, and community flare-ups where we had different gangs and teenage groups that triggered tension and physical conflicts. Some of these came from other communities. We were able to work as a team with stakeholders to change that environment to one of harmony, safety, and prosperity.

It is now a school that is sought after by many. Parents no longer worry about the perception of violence and feel safe sending their children to school. We have come a remarkable distance and have made significant steps in the right direction. We are seriously engaged with the diaspora. We have achieved much in terms of infrastructure and development. Former students have contributed immensely to the school, especially the bathroom facilities and our feeding programs. Programs have been designed to bring in care packages and other necessary items that serve the students and the wider community.

Our school has come a long way. One of its achievements is the first high school in Westmoreland to purchase a school bus to transport those who live far from school. Little London High School has seen many improvements from 2012 to the present. We now operate two centers at the external examination level, meaning the exams are administered by an exam body outside of the school's jurisdiction and can either be exam bodies that are external nationally or internationally, something that did not exist before 2012. We are also in a system that allows us to manage and operate in collaboration with the Caribbean Examinations Council.

Remarkably, the Global Humanity Network Organization came on board and transformed our Physical Education Department. We will be able to launch a very effective and robust program in September

2023 to engage the students in sporting activities, such as track and field, football, cricket, and netball among others. We want everyone to take advantage of the opportunity of being the next Usain Bolt, Shelly-Ann Fraser-Pryce, or any top-achieving athlete. We are ensuring that we fulfill and live our purpose so it can positively benefit the students.

My Political Work Serves My Purpose

I have been provided an excellent opportunity to live in my purpose through service. I am the steward of a wide section of Westmoreland that extends into Little Bay to Jerusalem and to areas of Negril. The opportunities there are enormous. I get to interface with so many individuals. I hear their concerns and suggestions and can guide them in directions that can be used to address their needs, especially some of the infrastructural problems they face.

As a councillor, I have successfully identified several routes within the division that were in a state of disrepair and were able to get the necessary funding to have these roads rehabilitated. Without that opportunity as a councillor, I would not be able to have impacted those communities in that way. I was able to assist the community of Jerusalem, among others, in getting potable water where access was available. Though it is not actually where it should be, it is still better than where it was before. Social programs within some communities have been expanded, facilitating access to overseas work programs. This opportunity allows them to give better support to their families as they may require.

The Covid 19 pandemic helped me to identify some of the most vulnerable people within our society. I have been able to contribute food items and care packages to those both far and near. It might never be enough, but it certainly was helpful in allowing individuals to save money to offset other expenses. For several years, some communities have not received any support from garbage collection. Being able to live in the most fulfilling area of my purpose, I can resolve that and put in the necessary infrastructure in terms of equipment and service support to ensure the environment in those areas remains safe. I have significantly worked with communities to uplift them. This is another remarkable opportunity to serve, live, and fulfill my purpose. And that's what I've been doing and will continue to do.

I entered representational politics in the year 2016 and was elected Councillor for Sheffield Division. It's a mixed economy within the division. Many of the locals are employed directly in the tourism industry in hotels in the Negril area. Some individuals are farming. Owing to the decline in the sugar industry and the fact that elderly individuals are no longer cultivating crops or rearing animals, many farmlands are now being used for housing development. The youths are now being encouraged to see farming as a career path.

Transportation plays a vital role in any economy, and as such, many individuals from Sheffield Division are engaged in the transport industry. In addition, fishing, carpentry, masonry, and small businesses are among some of the economic activities within the division.

However, there are still areas I need to tap into. It's something that I need to look carefully at and explore ways to ensure that there is an increase in opportunities for youngsters by diversifying the economy so that more people can access support services.

The Call for My Bid to Become a Member of Parliament

I have been encouraged by many people to vie for candidate selection as Member of Parliament (MP) Aspirant for the constituency of Western Westmoreland. This did not come as a result of friendship or by relationship, but by the good leadership qualities I possess, because of the work that I have done and am still doing, and by the value I placed on everyone as I live my life serving people. The fact is this is a bigger call to serve a bigger purpose. I have accepted the call because it will provide the opportunity where I will not be limited to a division but be able to impact the lives of an entire constituency and work with the people I love and care about. I know I will make a better mark on the constituency through teamwork and concerted effort as we create greater opportunities, resolve more problems, and improve the quality of life for all constituents. As I continue my work, I will enable the youths to find and pursue their destiny. This will foster better communities and ultimately a better country.

As I continue to uphold the tremendous responsibility to guide individuals, especially youths in the right direction, I look toward both short-term and long-term goals. I will continue to target infrastructure such as potable water distribution, expansion of rural electricity, and recreational activities that will help to stifle the monster of crime and violence, making the community one that is safe and comfortable to live in. There are great opportunities for community development and community programs for building and farming locally. And in general, to market the constituency as a place with great opportunities for investment, living, and raising families.

With greater emphasis placed on areas that will enhance development, the constituency will be able to cut import bills by producing food crops, securing markets, trading with neighboring parishes, building factories to deal with surpluses, and preserving goods for future use. Although these may constitute simple to complex problems, we will work together to find solutions to alleviate unfavorable situations as they arise.

Healthcare is of paramount importance to our community. We will certainly have healthy individuals if we have good healthcare. So, my plan is to find health facilities that need assistance and seek sponsorship with the vision that all constituents will be able to fairly access health services. We need to treat the population well. We should consider expanding those facilities to keep up with the increase in the population. Not all have access to it, and people from neighboring parishes will be looking for the same care. We should also consider constructing another hospital to create the needed balance.

The current leadership carries out basic roles and responsibilities, but more is needed. It could be more effective, and there is room for improvement across all sectors. Due to my involvement in administration, I am aware of the problems of crime, poor infrastructure, healthcare, and unemployment, as mentioned before.

There are so many shortfalls in these areas, and we need to see the type of proposals put forward that would be the policies necessary to drive these changes.

When I see the recommendations coming out, such as those that relate to a crime plan for the parish, I see it as an excellent plan for the country, but there needs to be individual plans for the communities within the parish. It would be best to have a plan for the constituency which would, by extension, benefit the country. I am not seeing these coming forward as solid points to launch the type of programs that are needed in the short and long term to start addressing some of the challenges that we are faced with under our new administration and new leadership from the Members of Parliament standpoint, and I believe strongly that these are some of the policies that need to be looked at.

I wish to bring it to the forefront, get stakeholders' engagement, and have discussions so that the people understand them clearly. If we have a crime plan for our parish and for our constituency and the constituents are cognizant of this and the role they will play, then it can be effective. We also need all the stakeholders on board. These are some critical areas the current administration could improve.

We need to see the type of investment that impacts the infrastructure of the constituency. When I see poor infrastructure, and I look at the amount of money that leaves the parish in terms of taxation against what comes back as investment, I realize the disparity is huge, and must be carefully examined.

Negril, one of the top tourism communities in the country, contributes significant revenue; but the community does not benefit much from this. There should be a decision taken on the amount of revenue collected from each parish that a percentage remains there to maintain that parish so that there will not be an overrun, allowing the parish itself to benefit from its income.

Investing In Our Resources

I believe we should invest in our resources. I have investigated some areas, and there are others, through collaboration with the constituents, I will pursue. This will add value for individuals in my constituency as well as further enable my purpose. I will continue to serve, especially when I see the changes that my purpose brings to the lives of others. It is a remarkable opportunity given to me.

Whoever becomes exposed to my story, I encourage you to never cease to live your purpose but walk with strength and dignity in your purpose because the inner rewards are great. Failure to do so could rob you of being who you are, where you should be, and deny other individuals the opportunity of experiencing blessings through your purpose. Living one's purpose is necessary for the continuity of a good society.

How I Want to Be Remembered

I want to be remembered as one who succeeded in achieving his purpose. And because I did not fail to live my purpose, I was able to impact the lives of others to be the best they can as they walk in their purpose. So, I want to be remembered as someone who fulfilled my purpose and ultimately and directly lived my destiny.

Because, in essence, my purpose is my destiny. So, I must ensure that my purpose impacts the lives of others in a very positive way. I want readers to take from my story that in living your purpose, you need to be true to yourself. If you are not being true to yourself, it means you are not living your true purpose.

If you realize that you are on a path that serves only to hurt others, that does not provide opportunities for others to uplift themselves, is not beneficial to you or those around you, then you need to reassess, re-evaluate the situation, and see if you are being true to yourself. Ask yourself: Am I truly living my purpose? Is this my real purpose? Find your true purpose and continue to shine and be the best you can.

Purpose that is well served is a purpose that positively impacts others. Indeed, I want everyone to understand how critical it is in your daily activities. And if you disagree with me, ask someone or have someone ask you to define the word purpose. If you take the opportunity to do that, you will realize that the word purpose has been with you since you came into this world. A word that is simple, yet complex.

While it is simple, complex, and critical, it is crucial for all of us, despite our educational background and the errors made while carrying out what we may choose to be, whether rich or poor. It is a concept that we all should ensure that we understand. Because if we serve our purpose, we will succeed in doing what is right at the end of the day, and it will continue to motivate me so that I can always live my purpose in the best possible way through honesty and integrity. So let us all continue to live our purpose. God bless you.

About The Visionary Author

Dr. Laxley W. Stephenson, a renowned scholar, consultant, and certified life navigation coach, is celebrated for his transformative work in guiding individuals to discover their purpose and overcome adversity. As CEO of A Collision With Purpose, he uses his empathetic approach and innate connection with others to help them realize their unique life purposes. Dr. Stephenson holds a Doctor of Business Administration degree in Leadership, is passionate about empowering youth, and is an avid advocate for social change. His unwavering dedication to personal growth has made him a guiding light in self-improvement. Through his speaking engagements and philanthropic efforts, he inspires countless people to embrace their pain, seize their destinies, and overcome obstacles to purposeful living. Dr. Stephenson's devotion to service is evident as President and CEO of Global Humanity Network, Inc. His non-profit organization supports underprivileged youth by offering resources and aid, enabling them to pursue their dreams and lead purpose-driven lives.

www.ingramcontent.com/pod-product-compliance
Lightning Source LLC
Chambersburg PA
CBHW051524050726
47503CB00014B/1313